DURCH STARTEN

ENGLISCH

BHS-MATURA

13

TESTBUCH

SCHÜLERiNNENAUSGABE

Verfasserinnen: Margot Benko und Erika Maria Benko

Diesem Buch ist ein Lösungsheft zu den Übungen beigelegt.

Entspricht der Rechtschreibreform 2006

Bibliografische Information der Deutschen Bibliothek:
Die Deutsche Bibliothek verzeichnet diese Publikation in der Deutschen Nationalbibliografie; detaillierte bibliografische Daten sind im Internet über http://dnb.ddb.de abrufbar.

VERITAS-VERLAG, Linz
www.durchstarten.at

Lektorat: Klaus Kopinitsch
Bildredaktion: Alexandra Rittberger
Textredaktion: Elisabeth Maureder
Grafische Gestaltung: Gottfried Moritz
Illustrationen: Helmut »Dino« Breneis
Satz: Toni Froschauer
Herstellung: Julia Dresch
Gedruckt in Österreich auf umweltfreundlich hergestelltem Papier

2. Auflage 2013
ISBN 978-3-7058-8978-1

VERITAS

Gemeinsam besser lernen

TABLE OF CONTENTS

INTRODUCTION

Liebe zukünftige Maturantin, lieber zukünftiger Maturant!

Bevor wir dir unser Buch ein bisschen näherbringen, möchten wir dir einmal recht herzlich zu all dem gratulieren, was du schon erreicht hast! Bald hat die Schulzeit ein Ende – und damit es ein Ende ganz ohne Schrecken ist, haben wir das vorliegende Testbuch für dich *designed*.
Durchstarten Englisch Testbuch für die neue BHS-Matura ist in erster Linie auf dich und deine Bedürfnisse zugeschnitten. Wenn du jedoch die Möglichkeit dazu hast, gemeinsam mit KollegInnen, LehrerInnen, Nachhilfe-lehrerInnen, *Native Speakers* und UnterstützerInnen aller Arten mit diesem Buch zu arbeiten, dann nütze sie unbedingt! Da es im sprachlichen Kontext beinahe immer um Kommunikation und Interaktion geht, möchten wir dich dazu einladen, diesen Prinzipien auch hier Folge zu leisten.

Buchaufbau

Jedes Kapitel ist gleich aufgebaut. Zuerst bieten wir dir zwei Übungen zum **Leseverständnis** (***Reading Comprehension***) und danach eine **Hörverständnisübung (*Listening Comprehension*)**. Darüber hinaus finden sich **Schreibaufträge** und **Übungen zur Vorbereitung auf die mündliche Matura** am Ende jedes Kapitels.

Wir haben diese Kapitel zusammengestellt, um dir die Möglichkeit zu bieten, so viel wie möglich zu üben und zu trainieren. Manche Aufgaben sind aus Übungszwecken überdurchschnittlich lang. Bei deiner schriftlichen Matura wirst du daher von der eigentlichen Kürze der Aufgaben positiv überrascht sein!

Was die Prüfungsformate und Methoden betrifft, so haben wir nur jene verwendet, die den Richtlinien der soge-nannten **Standardisierten Reifeprüfung** entsprechen. Wir sind daher fest davon überzeugt, dass du dich mit Hilfe unserer Übungen und Testaufgaben optimal auf deine große Prüfung vorbereiten kannst!

Ab Seite 66 findest du zwei **Probematuren**. Matura 1 und Matura 2 sind genauso aufgebaut, wie es deine Matura sein wird. Du kannst also deine Fähigkeiten und Kenntnisse noch einmal überprüfen! Nütze auch den Notenschlüssel, den wir dir bereitgestellt haben, um genau evaluieren zu können, was du schon alles kannst und was du vielleicht noch ein bisschen üben solltest. Da wir die *Writing Tasks* und auch die mündlichen Aufgabenstellungen nicht beurteilen können, haben wir diese Teile auch nicht in unsere Probematuren inkludiert.

Testformate

■ Reading Comprehensions und Listening Comprehensions

Wenn du die jeweilige Aufgabenstellung genau liest, wirst du keine Probleme damit haben zu verstehen, wie die Aufgabe zu lösen ist. Darüber hinaus haben wir zu jeder Aufgabenstellung mindestens ein Probebeispiel angeführt.

Die Fragen, die mit „Q plus einer Zahl“ (Q1, Q2, Q3 ...) gekennzeichnet sind, folgen stets dem natürlichen Verlauf des Textes, auf den sie sich beziehen. Es geht also alles schön der Reihe nach! ☺

Zudem haben wir am Ende jeder Aufgabenstellung Platz für deine Antworten bereitgestellt.

Die Hörtexte findest du auf der beiliegenden CD. Solltest du keine Möglichkeit haben, die CD abzuspielen, dann bitte einfach FreundInnen oder Bekannte, dir den Text vorzulesen. Die Transkripte aller Hörtexte findest du im Lösungsheft.

Du kannst dich auch benoten. Rechne einfach mit einem Punkt pro richtiger Antwort, addiere danach die erreichten Punkte und verwende das auf der rechten Seite angeführte Punktesystem:

Progress Check 1		
Points		Grade
from	to	
25	24	1
23	21	2
20	18	3
17	15	4
14	0	5

Progress Check 2		
Points		Grade
from	to	
22	21	1
20	19	2
18	16	3
15	13	4
12	0	5

Progress Check 3		
Points		Grade
from	to	
27	25	1
24	22	2
21	19	3
18	16	4
15	0	5

Progress Check 4		
Points		Grade
from	to	
23	22	1
21	20	2
19	17	3
16	14	4
13	0	5

Progress Check 5		
Points		Grade
from	to	
19	18	1
17	16	2
15	14	3
13	11	4
10	0	5

Progress Check 6		
Points		Grade
from	to	
28	26	1
25	23	2
22	20	3
19	17	4
16	0	5

■ Writing Tasks

Auch hier ist es wichtig, dass du die Aufgabenstellung genau liest, bevor du dich an die Arbeit machst. Grundsätzlich besteht jede *Writing Task Section* aus drei Schreibaufträgen (A, B, C).

■ Speaking Tasks

Obwohl die mündlichen Aufgabenstellungen selbstverständlich nicht Teil deiner schriftlichen Matura sein werden, haben wir diese dennoch in das vorliegende Testbuch aufgenommen, um dir auch hinsichtlich deiner Vorbereitung auf die mündliche Reifeprüfung ein bisschen unter die Arme greifen zu können. Selbst wenn du dich diesen Aufgaben alleine – also ohne KommunikationspartnerIn – stellst, möchten wir dich dazu ermutigen, dir mögliche Konversationen vorzustellen und laut vorzusprechen.

Manchmal bieten wir dir in unseren *Speaking Task Sections* auch Rollenspiele an. Auch diese solltest du verbal umsetzen, auch wenn du alleine arbeitest. So wirst du im Endeffekt nicht nur genug Übung im Sprechen, sondern auch das nötige Selbstvertrauen aufgebaut haben.

■ Question Time

Wir bieten dir auch sogenannte *Question Time Sections* an. Diese werden nicht Teil deiner eigentlichen Matura sein. Wir haben sie in unser Buch aufgenommen, um dir dabei zu helfen, dich selbst einzuschätzen, dein Wissen zu überprüfen und dich durch deine Lernerfahrungen zu führen.

■ Keys

Lösungen zu allen Leseverständnisübungen und Hörverständnisübungen findest du im beigelegten Lösungsheft.

■ Transcripts

Wie bereits erwähnt, bieten wir dir auch alle Transkripte der Hörverständnisübungen. Diese befinden sich ebenfalls im beigelegten Lösungsheft.

■ Matura 1 und Matura 2

Kommen wir noch einmal auf die zwei Probematuren zu sprechen: Diese Probeprüfungen stellen Modelle der Teilprüfungen aus den Bereichen Lese- und Hörverständnis deiner schriftlichen Matura dar.

Diese beinhalten, im Gegensatz zu den sechs *Progress Checks*, keine *Writing* und *Speaking Task Sections*, da diese noch nicht Teil des standardisierten Paketes sind und ohne Hilfe einer Lehrerin/eines Lehrers weder evaluiert noch benotet werden können. Lösungen und Transkripte finden sich im beigelegten Lösungsheft, der Notenschlüssel auf Seite 65.

We are keeping our fingers crossed for you and your challenges ahead!

Keep smiling and rocking the language!

All the best on your way to GREAT SUCCESS!

Mag. Margot Benko & Mag. Erika Maria Benko

EXAM UPDATE 4 U

Unser Durchstarten-Service gratis für SIE!

Die Aufgaben- und Testformate der neuen, teilzentralisierten Reife- und Diplomprüfung befinden sich zum gegebenen Zeitpunkt noch in der Konzeptions- und Pilotierungsphase, d.h., sie stehen noch nicht in ihrer endgültigen Form fest. Für SchülerInnen ist es jedoch wichtig, sich so bald wie möglich mit diesen Formaten und Anforderungen auseinandersetzen zu können und gezielt auf ihre Abschlussprüfung auf GERS Niveau B2 hinzuarbeiten.

VERITAS bietet daher SchülerInnen und LehrerInnen ein einmaliges Durchstarten-Servicepaket an:

Die in dieser Lernhilfe angebotenen **prüfungsrelevanten Übungen** können nur den **derzeitigen Informationsstand** abbilden. Es handelt sich dabei um **vorbereitende Aufgabenstellungen**, nicht endgültige Testformate. Um über die **aktuellen Entwicklungen** am Laufenden gehalten zu werden, **registrieren Sie sich online und erhalten Sie GRATIS per E-Mail**

- **Informationen** zum laufenden Stand der Entwicklungen der standardisierten Reifeprüfung,
- **Informationen** zu eventuellen Änderungen der Testformate,
- **Aufgaben** und **Übungsmöglichkeiten** zu den entsprechenden neuen/geänderten Formaten.

Wir hoffen, Sie mit diesem Service noch besser bei der Vorbereitung auf Ihre Matura unterstützen zu können, und wünschen Ihnen jetzt schon viel Erfolg und gutes Gelingen!

Registrierung unter: www.durchstarten.at/registrierung/9783705889781

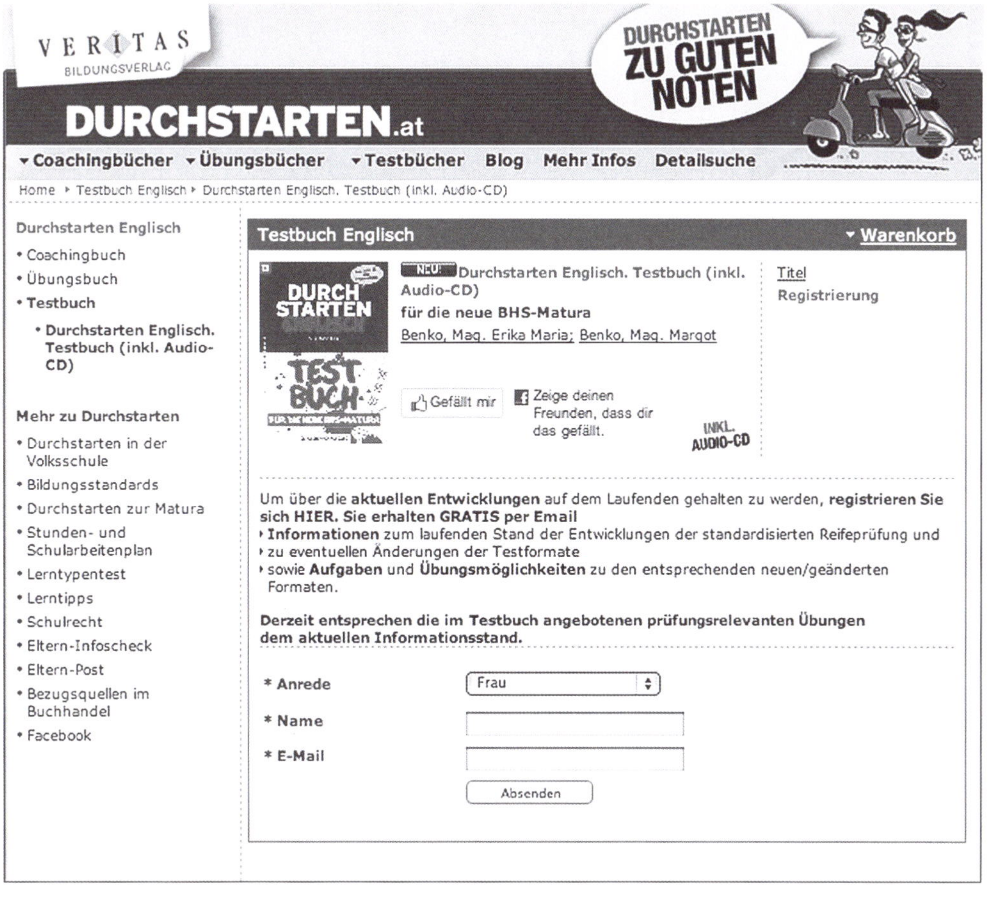

TIME FRAME
20 min

Progress Check 1: ART & ARCHITECTURE

Reading Comprehension 1

You are going to read the article "£430 million art stolen in 'heist[1] of the century'". However, some parts of the text are missing. Choose the correct answer (A–K) for each gap (Q1–Q9). There is one extra part that does not belong to the article at all. Write your answers in the boxes below. We have done the first example (0) for you.

£430 million art stolen in "heist of the century"
By Peter Allen and Justin Davenport

Masterpieces worth up to £430 million, (0) ____________, have been stolen during an audacious [...] raid[2] on a Paris museum.

Thieves broke into the city's Museum of Modern Art in a robbery described by the police as the "art heist of the century". The thieves (Q1) ____________ sophisticated[3] alarm systems and broken into the heavily protected building in the early hours. Staff spotted the theft when they arrived for work at 7am today. In total, five great works were taken. One police source said: "It's an enormous crime – one of the biggest in art history. The paintings are estimated (Q2) ____________ £500 million."

A man was captured on CCTV[4] as he climbed through a museum window. "He (Q3) ____________ a hood and face covering", said an officer. Sensors suggested that the window was smashed at 6.50 am. A security lock inside the building had also been broken. Police and art investigators have cordoned off[5] the building, just across the river Seine from the Eiffel Tower, and are studying CCTV footage. The paintings stolen are Picassos's Pigeon With Green Peas; Matisse's Pastoral; George Braque's Landscape With Olive Tree; Amadeo Modigliani's Woman With A Fan and Ferdinand Leger's Still Life With A Chandelier.

Experts said they would be impossible to sell on the open market. Art critic Louis Maillot said: "These paintings could never be sold, they would be spotted instantly. The usual scenario is that these things are stolen to order for private collectors. They are very (Q4) ____________ is enormous."

Until now, the biggest (Q5) ____________ was a raid on the Isabella Stewart Gardner Museum in Boston in 1990. Then, thieves disguised as police talked their way into the museum before handcuffing security guards and stealing over 13 works of art valued at over £500 million, a Vermeer and three works by Rembrandt van Rijn. The paintings have never been found.

---

1 heist: Raub, Raubüberfall
2 audacious raid: kühner Überraschungsangriff
3 sophisticated: ausgeklügelt, hochentwickelt
4 CCTV (closed-circuit television): Überwachungskamera
5 to cordon off: abriegeln

France has long been at the centre of the international art theft underworld, with paintings – (Q6) ____________ – being regularly stolen [...]. Galleries including the Orsay on the Left Bank and the Picasso on the Right Bank have been targeted regularly. Insiders working in the galleries for low pay (Q7) ____________ the criminals. The Museum of Modern Art in Paris, which is dedicated to 20th Century Art, is meant to be one of the most secure in the world.

British art crime investigator Dick Ellis, director of Art Management Group, said: "If these estimates of the value are true then this could be the biggest theft in history.

The (Q8) ____________ are less unique than those taken from the Gardner Museum but their total value may be more. The trend of museum thefts recently has been for criminals to go in when the museums are open to the public. The fact that this museum was robbed while it was closed suggests it was a professional and sophisticated theft. They clearly defeated the alarm systems."

Julian Radcliffe, chairman of the Art Loss Register, said: "The criminals weigh up the risk-profit ratio[1]. To (Q9) ____________ of the high degree of security so they are attracted to a museum [...]."

A	... to be worth
B	... particularly Picassos
C	... unsolved art theft in history
D	... was heavily disguised with
E	... including works by Picasso and Matisse
F	... paintings stolen
G	... difficult to value but the price
H	... cannot get that much money
I	... steal cash of this amount is impossible because
J	... are understood to have defeated
K	... are often suspected of helping

9 points
(1 point each)

0	Q1	Q2	Q3	Q4	Q5	Q6	Q7	Q8	Q9
E									

[1] risk-profit ratio: das Verhältnis zwischen Risiko und Profit

TIME FRAME
20 min

Reading Comprehension 2 ✓

You are going to read the article "Sky's the limit". Read the text carefully. Then complete the sentences (Q10–Q17) by using a maximum of 4 words. Write your answers in the spaces provided. We have done the first example (0) for you.

Sky's the limit
£85m Battle of Britain monument revealed
By Kevin Bradford

A massive exhibition tower is set to become an iconic centrepiece for the Royal Air Force in Colindale. The proposed 350ft (116 metre) high monument would house a Battle of Britain exhibition and would be built on the RAF Museum[1] site, in Grahame Park Way.

It would eclipse[2] Big Ben and New York's Statue of Liberty, and would mark the "collective endeavour[3] of the British people" during the defining air battle in 1940. The £85 million steel and glass structure would feature aircrafts suspended from the clear ceiling along with interactive educational facilities and artefacts.

Air Vice-Marshal Peter Dye, the museum's new director-general, said the external aspects of the design are meant to represent the sky over London in 1940, while the exhibits will encapsulate[4] the spirit that came out of the conflict. He said: "We're not talking about a memorial here as much as it is a statement of what is important to the nation, to the RAF, and why the values of 1940 continue to be significant. [...] It's actually about why it continues to be important, and therefore the educational aspect is fundamental to the project. It will represent the values that have an enduring relevance as we realise the Battle of Britain had an enduring impact across the world."

Mr. Dye hopes the building will become as iconic for the RAF as Nelson's Column is for the Navy, and put Colindale on the international map.

The aim is to complete the development by the RAF's 75th anniversary celebrations, five years from now, to ensure it is opened while the remaining veterans of the conflict are still alive. "We want to do this now because the number of ex-servicemen is rapidly diminishing", said Mr Dye. "We really believe the time is right to create a building that celebrates, commemorates[5] and educates." [...]

Plans for the exhibition tower were unveiled[6] last week and the formal planning process is now underway.

The buildings would dominate the skyline around the museum in Grahame Park Way, and could be seen as too imposing by people living nearby. But Air Vice-Marshal Peter Dye, the museum's director-general, said he hopes residents will realise the aim of the development is to explain the heritage of the area they live in. [...]

Trustees at the museum, along with designers and architects, are putting together a formal planning application to present to Barnet Council. And Mr. Dye said representatives from the museum had already been in contact with council officers. He said: "We have started to express to local organisations and agencies what our vision is and what we are trying to show to the wider community, what we are trying to achieve. There is very strong public interest in this and the planning process will hopefully tease all those views out."

---

[1] RAF Museum: Royal Air Force Museum
[2] to eclipse: in den Schatten stellen
[3] endeavour: Bemühen, Anstrengung
[4] to encapsulate: auf den Punkt bringen
[5] to commemorate: in Erinnerung bringen
[6] to unveil: enthüllen, darlegen

Mr. Dye said there had been a "very positive reaction" to the design. [...] He said: "It will not only be an impressive building but an iconic building. But that in itself raises issues in terms of the scale of the environment. We need to address all kinds of aspects, such as transportation, and this will be part of the planning process. We need to understand what impact that is going to have."

0	Inside the exhibition tower, the Battle of Britain exhibition ________.	**would be housed**
Q10	The highly expensive exhibition tower would be made out of ________.	
Q11	The exterior design of the tower shall symbolize the ________.	
Q12	The project's purpose is to show the continuing significance of ________.	
Q13	The tower shall be built and completed very soon so that it can be opened while many ex-servicemen ________.	
Q14	Mr. Dye believes that it is the right time for a monumental building that ________.	
Q15	People who live in the area will hopefully understand that the project aims at explaining the ________.	
Q16	At the moment architects, designers and trustees are working on a ________.	
Q17	According to Mr. Dye people have reacted positively ________.	

8 points
(1 point each)

Question Time: "Sky´s the limit"

Reflect on the text and answer the questions below.

- What do we learn about the design of the planned exhibition tower?
- What might the neighbours think about the building?
- What is your opinion on the project?

TIME FRAME
15 min

Listing Comprehension

CD-TRACK 01

You are going to hear a report about an art project called "Imagine Art After". You have 45 seconds to read the sentences below before the text will be played to you twice. While listening, choose the correct answer (A, B, C or D) for each statement (Q1–Q8). Put an ✗ in the correct box. We have done the first example (0) for you. After you have listened to the text twice, you will have another 45 seconds to go through your answers again.

Imagine Art After

0 The Guardian helped setting up the project "Imagine Art After"

A	in 2009.	
B	in 2005.	✗
C	in 2010.	
D	in 1996.	

Q1 The "Imagine Art After" project was carried out

A	by 7 British artists.	
B	by 14 artists all together.	
C	by 7 artists from various troubled regions.	
D	by various British newspapers.	

Q2 Two years ago the artists were invited to

A	start talking to their project partners online and to share ideas.	
B	meet each other and create art together.	
C	work for the Guardian's talk boards.	
D	introduce themselves to the world with the help of online platforms.	

Q3 The person who developed the project

A	is a film maker.	
B	is a film star.	
C	is interested in castings.	
D	wanted "Imagine Art After" to be a film project.	

Q4 The person who developed the project selected artists and

A	paired them together according to their CVs.	
B	paired them together following her instincts only.	
C	paired them together considering artistic similarities, personalities, and her own instinct.	
D	paired them together taking only their artistic similarities into account.	

Q5 The girl from Iraq who has been living in London for a long time

A	was paired up with a young Iraqi artist.	
B	was paired up with a nearly 40 year old Iraqi artist.	
C	was paired up with a nearly 50 year old Kurdish artist from Iraq.	
D	was paired up with a nearly 40 year old Kurdish artist from Iraq.	

Q6 The two Iraqi artists (Iraqi/Kurdish)

A	were very similar with regard to their art.	
B	were artistically not similar at all.	
C	were both very political in their art.	
D	were both quite abstract in the way they painted.	

Q7 The Afghanistan dialogue

A	was very successful.	
B	was very much about two men passionately discussing their family lives.	
C	worked out well enough.	
D	was rather a set of two monologues than a real dialogue.	

Q8 The dialogue between the two Serbian artists

A	often developed significantly overnight.	
B	was ignored by many people.	
C	encouraged people to stay home from work.	
D	was not very successful either.	

8 points
(1 point each)

TOTAL
POINTS

Writing

Write all three of the required texts (A, B and C).

A. Report (250 words, +/-10%)

Your teacher is organizing a school project on Art and Education and has asked you to write a report about your classmates' views on the importance of art and creativity. You have already started working on it by talking to your friends and by taking the following notes.

ART & CREATIVITY

students in class: 33
cooperative students in class: 28

art is very important: 17
creativity is important: 19

★ – **art is important because:**
- good for fantasy and imagination
- mirrors reality: good and bad things
- is beautiful, inspires us

★ – **creativity is important because:**
- helps us solve problems
- makes lives easier and happier
- is natural (kids)

You are now ready to write a report based on your notes that will inform the readers about your survey and will discuss the results. Do not forget to divide your report into sections and to come up with an appropriate heading for each of them.

Don't forget to
- give information about your survey
- discuss the findings
- make suggestions with regard to art and creativity projects in classrooms

Write approximately 250 words.

B. E-mail (250 words, +/-10%)

You are the editor-in-chief of your school magazine "AAA". The members of your team have been quite lazy lately and have shown little motivation. You have also not received any articles for quite a while. As your anniversary issue is soon due, you are getting a little bit nervous. Write an e-mail to everybody in your team,
- discussing their obvious lack of motivation
- stating your wishes and requests
- suggesting a proper work plan for the near future

Write around 250 words.

C. Blog Post (250 words, +/-10%)

You are doing an internship at an architect's office in London (page 15) at the moment. As your friends at home are really curious and want to know as much as possible about your daily work life in London, you have promised to set up a blog for them to read.

In your blog you should
- describe your daily tasks and duties
- inform them about your workplace and about your colleagues
- present general impressions about living and working abroad

Write about 250 words. Don't forget to give your blog a title.

***Company**: B. o. B. London*

Internship description:

- *working with Autocad Design*
- *Office, Photoshop, Internet, PowerPoint, Filemaker*

Requirements:

- *degree in architecture*
- *to be dedicated, creative, hard-working*
- *very good language skills*
- *open-minded, out-going, teamplayer*
- *driver's license, first aid certificate*

***Salary**: 650$ a month*
***Start date**: 1st of July*
***Duration**: 1 to 3 months*

***Industry**: Architecture*
***Region/City**: London, UK*
***Category**: internship*
***Mode of employment**: 5 hours/day*
***Contract type**: temporary*

Speaking

A. WORK IN PAIRS: Discuss the following quotations:

- What are the following quotations about?
- Do you agree with what is said?
- Use the quotations as a starting point for a discussion.

Creativity is allowing yourself to make mistakes. Art is knowing which ones to keep.
(Scott Adams)

Painting is just another way of keeping a diary.
(Pablo Picasso)

Painting is poetry that is seen rather than felt, and poetry is painting that is felt rather than seen.
(Leonardo da Vinci)

All art requires courage.
(Anne Tucker)

There are three forms of visual art: Painting is art to look at, sculpture is art you can walk around, and architecture is art you can walk through.
(Dan Rice)

An architect is the drawer of dreams.
(Grace McGarvie)

Architecture is music in space, as if it were a frozen music.
(Friedrich Wilhelm Joseph von Schelling)

B. Individual Task

1. Architecture

Have a look at the two photographs below. Compare and contrast them, and give your opinion about them. Imagine you are talking to a large audience that you are trying to impress. Watch your body language, your gestures, your facial expression, and your language. You have three minutes. Try to keep talking and to avoid any long gaps. Start by describing what you can actually see and then continue by comparing, contrasting, and interpreting.

MEV Verlag/Cornelius Scheidter

Shotshop.com/Scout

2. Art

Have a look at the two paintings below. Compare and contrast them, and give your opinion about them. Imagine again you are talking to a large audience that you are trying to impress. Watch your body language, your gestures, your facial expression, and your language. You have three minutes. Try to keep talking and to avoid any long gaps. Start by describing what you can actually see and then continue by comparing, contrasting, and interpreting.

akg-images/Juan Gris

picturedesk.com/Toni Schneiders/Interfoto/Hans Leonhard Schäufelein

Progress Check 2: EXPLORING THE WORLD

TIME FRAME
20 min

Reading Comprehension 1

You are going to read the article "Our man in Iran" from the Guardian. Read the text carefully and decide whether the statements (Q1–Q8) in the box below are true (T) or false (F). Mark the correct answer with an ✗. Furthermore, justify your answer by quoting the first 4 words of the sentence that gives away the answer (T or F) and write it in the column "Justification". We have done the first example (0) for you.

Our man in Iran
By Christopher Dobbing

The gap year is essentially a 14-month break in the warm, fuzzy space between education and the real world. After the obligatory crummy jobs[1], and scrimping[2] and saving for months, I'd got enough together for a 90-day round-the-world trip, including 10 days crossing Iran.
I was travelling alone on the regular overland bus service between London and Sydney, Ozbus. The three-month journey crosses 18 countries and every imaginable terrain. For me, though, Iran was the appeal. I'm fascinated by the place. It's one of the cradles of civilisation. President Ahmadinejad has put the country at the centre of world politics, and I went to see what all the fuss is about.
After leaving Turkey, the bus took us from Tabriz in the north-west to Bam in the south-east. I was overwhelmed by how different everything was from my expectations. Everywhere the streets are buzzing. Everyone seemed contented and cheerful, and those who spoke any English often came up for a chat. It gave the country a brilliant, friendly feel. […] I felt safe and welcomed.
As I gazed at a shop window one day at a magnificent array of silver trinkets, I was approached by a young Iranian guy of about my age, who introduced himself as Ali. We chatted for a while. He playfully came out with a load of cockney rhyming slang he'd learned from some Brits who had passed through a couple of months before. Impressed, I asked what he did for a living. He pulled a face. "If I tell you, you'll run away." I cautiously promised not to. Ali looked at me, grinned and declared: "I'm a carpet seller." I burst into laughter, and so did he. He took me to his shop, gave me tea and we talked about the country. Not once did he mention buying a carpet. From my conversations with him, I got the impression that politics was very detached from the streets, the upcoming elections were of little interest to Ali or any of his family or friends. […]
One day, Ali explained, he would like to go to Australia and start a business there, but he would never get a passport. To be granted permission to leave the country, Iranian citizens must do two years' national service, something that he refused to do. My British passport was burning a hole in my pocket at this point, and I felt guilty for my right to travel wherever the whim[3] took me.
The trip gave me a new respect for the freedoms I had, an appreciation of our multicultural and liberal way of life, and experience of doing my own laundry. I'd recommend a gap year to anyone.

---

[1] crummy jobs: miese Jobs
[2] to scrimp: an allen Enden sparen
[3] wherever the whim took me: … ganz nach Lust und Laune

	Statements	T	F	Justification
0	People go on a gap year after school and before they start a real job.	✘		The gap year is …
Q1	Christopher Dobbing was saving money until he had enough for his round-the-world adventure.			
Q2	Christopher Dobbing travelled with friends.			
Q3	Christopher Dobbing had always thought of Iran as a buzzing country.			
Q4	Ali and Christopher Dobbing met in front of a shop.			
Q5	It was especially silver trinkets that Ali sold.			
Q6	Ali did not seem to be highly interested in politics.			
Q7	Ali dreamt of going abroad one day.			
Q8	Christopher Dobbing's pocket tore and had a hole.			

8 points
(1 point each)

Question Time: "Our man in Iran"

Reflect on the text and answer the questions below.

- What do we learn about Christopher Dobbing's journey?
- Which impressions of Iran and its people do you get?
- Would you like to go on a gap year? If yes, why? If no, why not?

TIME FRAME
20 min

Reading Comprehension 2

You are going to read an article about Vietnam. Read the text carefully and decide for each sentence (Q9–Q15) which answer (A, B, C or D) is the correct one. Put an ✗ in the correct box. We have done the first example (0) for you.

Vietnam: Along the Mekong
A river runs through it
By Justine Southwick

The Mekong Delta is a complex maze of waterways and is the rice bowl of Vietnam. Travelling on a Kumuka tour, Justine Southwick cruises into the heart of the region, viewing life as the local population does. A [...] man of indefinable age, a cigarette dangling from his mouth as he checks his fishing nets, stops to stare at a boat puttering past[1]. Ramshackle[2] houses line the riverbank, where women busy themselves cooking or washing and children scamper[3] up and down. Everything looks exactly as I imagined it. I've only been in Vietnam three days, and my wide-eyed wonder has not yet given way to blasé[4] acceptance. I arrived in the Mekong region two days ago, fresh off the boat from the small town of Cai Be and ready to start my three-day tour. Cai Be is the gateway[5] to the inner delta region and a two-hour drive south from Ho Chi Minh City (Saigon to all but the country's government officials). Quan, my new guide, collects me from my hotel and we head south. Civilisation thins out as we bump our way down the dusty highway in a van. Industrial buildings give way to wooden shacks dotting[6] the roadside. [...] The smell of urine, so prevalent[7] in the city, is less evident here.
We leave the air-conditioned van to board a sampan – a Vietnamese river boat – bound for a rice-paper-making factory. Here I see people making pop rice (the Vietnamese version of popcorn). Back in the sampan, we round a bend in the river and the Mekong Delta opens up before me. It's huge and stretches west as far as Cambodia. It's also murky[8] brown, not fit for human consumption. Later, when I see men venturing out of their homes to dump their household rubbish into it, I realise why. Life here in southern Vietnam revolves around the Mekong River. At 4000 km in length it is, according to Quan, the world's eighth longest river. It starts in the Himalayas, flows through China, Myanmar, Laos, Thailand, Cambodia and Vietnam and has a different name in each country. The Vietnamese name, Song Cuu Long, means `river of nine dragons', so named for the nine mouths that lead to the sea. But to the locals it is known as the "mother river" because they depend on it for survival. These people live a tough life. Some live on boats, with no choice but to use the water for cooking and bathing. They eke out[9] an existence selling food or handcrafts and rarely set foot on land. They work so hard and have so little, yet they're the most generous, hospitable people I've come across. The Western World could learn a lot from them.

---

[1] to putter past: vorbeischaukeln
[2] ramshackle: baufällig, wackelig
[3] to scamper: herumhüpfen, hin und her huschen
[4] blasé: gelangweilt, gleichgültig
[5] gateway: Haupteinfahrt
[6] to dot: sprenkeln, stricheln, punktieren
[7] prevalent: vorherrschend
[8] murky: trüb
[9] to eke out: sich erkämpfen

Progress Check 2: EXPLORING THE WORLD

Quan cracks joke after joke as we continue to our lunch stop, a local homestead[1] surrounded by stunning gardens. Elephant ear fish, one of the region's delicacies, is served whole on a plate; I'm expected to pick it clean and make my own spring rolls following a demonstration by the woman who owns this place. I fail miserably. Dessert comprises tropical fruit such as ladyfinger bananas and agar, a jelly-like fruit that tastes like aniseed. [...].

0 The Mekong Delta

A	... is a very productive land thanks to the many waterways.	✗
B	... is a very dry area.	
C	... has many inhabitants who grow corn.	
D	... is especially known for its big lakes.	

Q9 On the bank

A	... of the river women are washing their children.	
B	... of the river women are cooking.	
C	... of the river women are looking after their children.	
D	... of the river women are busily playing with their children.	

Q10 Cai Be

A	... is situated in the south of Saigon.	
B	... is the gateway Ho Chi Minh City.	
C	... is situated in the centre of the inner delta region.	
D	... is the old name for Saigon.	

Q11 The traveller

A	... leaves the hotel to meet the tour guide.	
B	... meets his guide to discuss the next stages of the journey.	
C	... has known Quan for a long time.	
D	... gets picked up by the tour guide from his accommodation.	

Q12 The traveller

A	... encounters more and more people, who appear along the dusty road once they leave Cai Be.	
B	... encounters fewer and fewer people as they travel along a dusty road.	
C	... can see only a few wooden shacks alongside the dusty road.	
D	... believes that industrial buildings basically do not exist in Vietnam.	

---

[1] homestead: Ansiedelung

Q13 A sampan

A	… is a traditional Cambodian cruise ship.	
B	… needs a lot of pop rice.	
C	… takes the tourist and his guide to a rice-paper-making factory.	
D	… takes them all the way to Cambodia.	

Q14 The water

A	… is very clean.	
B	… is rather cold.	
C	… tempts people to jump into the river and take a swim.	
D	… of the river is quite polluted.	

Q15 The Mekong River

A	… is named "mother river" after Mother Theresa who lived there for nine months.	
B	… is called "mother river" by the locals as they desperately need it to survive their day-to-day lives.	
C	… translates into Song Cuu Long and this means "mother river".	
D	… is referred to as Song Cuu Long by the locals.	

7 points
(1 point each)

TIME FRAME
15 min

Listening Comprehension

CD-TRACK 02

You are going to hear parts of three famous songs.
You have 45 seconds to read the sentences below before the songs will be played to you twice. While listening, match the beginnings of the sentences (Q1–Q7) with the sentence endings (A–K). Write your answers in the table provided. There are three extra sentence endings that do not belong to the lyrics at all. We have done the first example (0) for you. After you have listened to the songs twice, you will have another 45 seconds to go through your answers again.

	1st song: Billy Joel: New York State of Mind
0	The singer states that there are people …
Q1	The singer himself rather …
Q2	Many stars …
Q3	For the singer, travelling further away from NY …
	2nd song: John Denver: Leaving on a jet plane
Q4	A man is standing in front of a house, …
Q5	He is very sad and asks his girlfriend to …
	3rd song: The Dubliners: Molly Malone
Q6	Molly Malone is a pretty girl …
Q7	Molly Malone's job was to …

A	… goes by Greyhound bus.
B	… kiss him and smile for him.
C	… who like flying away in the holiday season.
D	… is his wildest dream.
E	… appears to be a waste of time.
F	… about to get into a taxi to take him to the airport.
G	… sell mussels.
H	… possess big and expensive cars.
I	… own highly expensive outfits.
J	… from London, England.
K	… from Dublin, Ireland.

7 points
(1 point each)

0	Q1	Q2	Q3	Q4	Q5	Q6	Q7
C							

TOTAL POINTS

Writing

Write all three of the required texts (A, B and C).

A. E-mail (250 words, +/-10%)

Together with your class teacher, you and your classmates want to go on a trip to Italy for 12 days. As you have been out of the country twice already this year, you had to write a letter to your headmaster asking for permission to not attend the classes. However, your headmaster did not give you the permission to leave school again for another 12 days. Your teacher said that the first letter to the headmaster was too sloppy and was therefore rejected. You decide to write an e-mail, explaining the situation and asking for permission again.

In your e-mail you should:

- explain why you are writing
- discuss the educational advantages and general benefits of the planned trip to Italy
- offer an apology for your last letter

Write about 250 words.

B. Blog Post (250 words, +/-10%)

Your friend Max has asked you to help him with his father's blog. His father owns a flat on the beach of La Devesa, close to the beautiful city of Valencia, that he wants to rent out for the summer. You know the place very well as you spent your last holiday there.
Max has already put some photos and directions online. The only thing missing is an enthralling text, describing the beauty of the surrounding area, the city, and – of course – the flat itself. Your friend has provided you with the information and material below. Use the information to write an appealing and attractive blog post.

In your blog post you should:

- describe the place
- discuss the advantages of staying there
- present thoughts and reflections on your last holiday there

Write about 250 words. Don't forget to give your blog post a title.

Population Approx. 795,000 (city proper)
Autonomous Community La Comunidad de Valencia
People Valencianos
Languages Spanish and Valenciano/Valencià

Geography On Spain's mid-eastern Mediterranean coast
Climate Typically Mediterranean – mild winters and hot, dry summers
Average Yearly Temperature 21.5°C (70°F)

Local cuisine Valencia claims to be the birthplace of paella. The traditional regional style is saffron rice with chicken, rabbit, beans, snails and artichokes. There are more than 200 other rice dish varieties combining seafood, shellfish, game, vegetables and more.

THE FLAT:

75 m² living area • 4 people • 1 bedroom • 1 bathroom • elevator • air conditioning • internet access • radio • linen provided • 500 m from the beach

C. Report (250 words, +/-10%)

Tomorrow, a youth organization focusing on environmental and social issues, has invited young people to write reports on the effects tourism has on the environment on the one hand and on the lives of local communities on the other hand.
You have decided to send in a report you have written based on the text below.

1 Tourism is likely to create more jobs for your community.
2 Tourism is likely to attract more investment to your community.
3 Tourism is likely to provide more business for local people and small businesses.
4 Tourism is likely to create additional tax revenue from tourists for local governments.
5 High-spending tourists are likely to affect negatively our way of living.
6 Tourism is likely to change our local culture.
7 Local residents are likely to suffer from living in a tourism destination.
8 Tourism is likely to result in unpleasantly overcrowded beaches, walking paths, parks and outdoor places in your community.
9 Tourism is likely to put more pressure on local services such as police and fire protection, utilities, roads.
10 The cost of developing tourist facilities is too much.
11 Construction of hotels and other tourist facilities are likely to destroy the natural environment.
12 Tourism development is likely to provide an incentive for the restoration of historical buildings.
13 Tourism development is likely to provide an incentive for the conservation of natural resources.
14 Tourism development is likely to provide an incentive for the preservation of the local culture.
15 Our roads and other public facilities are likely to be kept at a high standard because of tourism.

In your report you should
- present your thoughts on the topic
- briefly summarize some of the statements above
- suggest how the tourism industry can adapt to today's environmental and social challenges

Write around 250 words. Structure your report properly and give each section a heading.

Speaking

A. WORK IN PAIRS: Discuss the following quotations:

- What are the following quotations about?
- Do you agree with what is said?
- Use the quotations as a starting point for a discussion.

The world is a book and those who do not travel read only one page.
(St. Augustine)

There are no foreign lands. It is the traveler only who is foreign.
(Robert Louis Stevenson)

People travel to faraway places to watch, in fascination, the kind of people they ignore at home.
(Dagobert D. Runes)

For my part, I travel not to go anywhere, but to go. I travel for travel's sake. The great affair is to move.
(Robert Louis Stevenson)

Twenty years from now you will be more disappointed by the things you didn't do than by the ones you did do. So throw off the bowlines, sail away from the safe harbor. Catch the trade winds in your sails. Explore. Dream. Discover.
(Mark Twain)

If you reject the food, ignore the customs, fear the religion and avoid the people, you might better stay at home.
(James Michener)

B. ROLE PLAY

This is a speaking task for a group of 3 candidates:
1 – the interlocutor, 2 – candidate A (Mary), 3 – candidate B (Sue)

Interlocutor's Sheet: You, as the interlocutor, know everybody and all the situations. Make sure you follow the discussion carefully and ask about certain aspects if they are not mentioned (see prompts).

This is what you tell the others at the beginning of the discussion:
Mary and Sue want to go on a gap year. They are both very excited and are about to make a proper plan as to where to go, when, how and for how long.
On your task sheet some impulses are provided. They have to be discussed but you can also talk about other aspects.

These are the prompts for the other candidates:

PROMPTS FOR CANDIDATE A:
You are Mary. You want to go on a gap year as you really need a time-out from everything. You have saved a bit of money and you hope that you will be able to work and make some more while travelling.

You know that Sue wants to come along and you are not sure if that is a good idea. You are really looking forward to the freedom and independence that will come along with your adventure.

Discuss:
- your ideas about your gap year
- your worries about being on the road together
- thoughts about freedom and independence
- your motivation to do it
- places you really want to see
- financial issues

PROMPTS FOR CANDIDATE B:
You are Sue. You have just finished school and as you are not sure about what to study, you decide to go on a gap year first. Your parents have already agreed and are willing to financially support you. You would love to join Mary and you hope that she will take care of you. You have basically promised your mum and dad that you will never travel by yourself and that you will always stay with Mary.

Discuss:
- your dream destinations
- why you want to go on a gap year
- that you do not want to be left alone in a foreign country
- your promise to mum and dad
- your financial situation

Role-card for candidate A: Gap Year

You are Mary. You want to go on a gap year as you really need a time-out from everything. You have saved a bit of money and you hope that you will be able to work and make some more while travelling.
You know that Sue wants to come along and you are not sure if that is a really good idea. You are really looking forward to the freedom and independence that will come along with your adventure.

Discuss:
- your ideas about your gap year
- your worries about being on the road together
- thoughts about freedom and independence
- your motivation to do it
- places you really want to see
- financial issues

Role-card for candidate B: Gap Year

You are Sue. You have just finished school and as you are not sure about what to study, you decide to go on a gap year first. Your parents have already agreed and are willing to financially support you. You would love to join Mary and you hope that she will take care of you. You have basically promised your mum and dad that you will never travel by yourself and that you will always stay with Mary.

Discuss:
- your dream destinations
- why you want to go on a gap year
- that you do not want to be left alone in a foreign country
- your promise to mum and dad
- your financial situation

Progress Check 3: EDUCATION & SOCIAL ISSUES

TIME FRAME
20 min

Reading Comprehension 1

You are going to read parts of the article "When does consciousness[1] arise?" However, some parts of the text are missing. Choose the correct answer (A–N) for each gap (Q1–Q12). There is one extra part that does not belong to the article at all. Write your answers in the boxes below. We have done the first example (0) for you.

When does consciousness arise?
In the womb[2], at birth or during early childhood?
By Christof Koch

Mothers will (0) ____________ me for this seemingly cruel question, but it needs to be posed: How do we know that a newly born and healthy infant is conscious? There is no question that the baby is awake. Its (Q1) ____________, it wriggles[3] and grimaces, and – (Q2) ____________ – it cries. But all that is not the same as being conscious, of experiencing pain, seeing red or smelling Mom's milk.

It is well recognized that infants have no awareness of their own state, emotions and motivations. Even (Q3) ____________ who can speak have very limited insight into their own actions. Anybody who has raised a boy is familiar with the blank[4] look on your teenager's face when you ask him why he did something particularly rash[5]. A shrug[6] and "I dunno – it seemed like a good idea at the time!" is the most you'll hear.

(Q4) ____________ a newborn lacks self-awareness, the baby processes complex visual stimuli[7] and attends to sounds and sights in its world, preferentially looking at faces. [...]

Linguistic capacities[8] in babies are shaped (Q5) ____________ in. Exposure to maternal speech sounds in the muffled confines[9] of the womb enables the fetus to pick up statistical regularities so that the newborn can (Q6) ____________ from others. A more complex behaviour is imitation: if dad sticks out his tongue and waggles it, the infant mimics his gesture by combining visual information with proprioceptive[10] feedback from its own movements. It is (Q7) ____________ the baby has some basic level of unreflective, present-oriented consciousness.

The Road to Awareness

But when does the magical journey of consciousness begin? Consciousness requires a sophisticated network of highly interconnected components, nerve cells. [...] Many of the circuit elements necessary for consciousness are in place by the third trimester.

(Q8) ____________, preterm infants can survive outside the womb under proper medical care. And as it is so much easier to observe and interact with a preterm baby than with a fetus, the fetus is often considered to be like a preterm baby, like an unborn newborn. [...]

---

[1] consciousness: Bewusstsein
[2] womb: Mutterleib
[3] to wriggle: sich winden
[4] blank: ausdruckslos, leer
[5] rash: übereilt, unbedacht
[6] shrug: Achselzucken
[7] visual stimuli: visuelle Reize
[8] linguistic capacities: sprachliche Fähigkeiten
[9] muffled confines: dumpfer Raum
[10] proprioceptive: propriozeptiv, eigene Reize wahrnehmend

Dreamless Sleep?

After birth, dream content is informed by recent and more remote[1] memories. Longitudinal studies[2] of dreaming in children by retired American psychologist David Foulkes suggest that (Q9) ____________ a gradual cognitive development that is tightly linked to the capacity to imagine things visually [...]. Thus, preschoolers' dreams are often static and plain, with no characters (Q10) ____________, hardly any feelings and no memories. What would dreaming be like for an organism that spends its time suspended in a sort of isolation tank, with no memories, and no way (Q11) ____________ at all? I wager[3] that the fetus experiences nothing in utero; that it feels the way we do when we are in (Q12) ____________ sleep.

The dramatic events attending delivery cause the brain to abruptly wake up, however. [...]
It draws its first breath, wakes up and begins to experience life.

A	... want to crucify
B	... therefore likely that
C	... older children
D	... distinguish its mother's voice and even her language
E	... most importantly
F	By this time ...
G	... dreaming is
H	Although ...
I	... by the environment they grow up
J	... wish to help
K	... that move or act
L	... eyes are wide open
M	... to imagine anything
N	... deep, dreamless

12 points
(1 point each)

0	Q1	Q2	Q3	Q4	Q5	Q6	Q7	Q8	Q9	Q10	Q11	Q12
A												

[1] remote: entfernt
[2] longitudinal studies: Langzeitstudien
[3] to wager: wetten

TIME FRAME
20 min

Reading Comprehension 2

You are going to read the article "Schools forced to 'mop up[1] social problems'" from the Daily Telegraph. Read the text carefully and decide whether the statements (Q13–Q19) in the box below are true (T) or false (F). Mark the correct answer with an ✗. Furthermore, justify your answer by quoting the first 4 words of the sentence that gives away the answer (T or F) and write it in the column "Justification". We have done the first example (0) for you.

Schools forced to "mop up social problems"

Schools are increasingly being forced to "mop up" social problems instead of focusing on traditional subjects, according to a charity founded by the Prince of Wales.

By Graeme Paton

An over-emphasis on issues such as obesity, drug abuse, teenage pregnancy, emotional literacy and bullying in the classroom have undermined the amount of time spent on rigorous academic study, it has been claimed. In a report, the Prince's Teaching Institute (PTI) said there were fears that a shift towards a "social rather than educational agenda[2]" in schools risked leaving children unprepared for the intellectual demands of university and the world of work.

Teachers said schools were being asked to encroach[3] into areas better left to parents or social workers. Some criticized a major policy document – "Every Child Matters" – launched[4] half way through the Labor government that spelt out 25 priorities for improving children's lives, but only two focused on education.

Bernice McCabe, director of the PTI and headmistress of the independent North London Collegiate School, said a recent conference staged by the charity underlined the extent to which teachers feared traditional subjects had been marginalized[5]. "There was wide agreement that many issues that dominate current thinking about the function of schools are more concerned with a social rather than educational agenda, and that the dissemination[6] of subject knowledge to the next generation is being diluted[7] as a result", she said.

A foreign language student at A-level may be asked to study poverty in inner cities rather than literature, Mrs McCabe suggested. She said that English Literature was more likely to be focused on a particular genre rather than the subject as a whole. "Because of the emphasis on skills and techniques, like 'learning to learn', and the inclusion of so many social imperatives such as health and social skills into the curriculum, children acquire less subject knowledge in schools and are less well prepared for the world of higher education", she said.

"If they train as teachers, they come back into the classroom with less confidence in their subject knowledge and very limited encouragement to develop it. And so the cycle is perpetuated[8]."

The PTI was founded by the Prince of Wales to encourage teachers to rediscover passion for their subjects. Earlier this year, it staged a seminar for head teachers on the issue of restoring "academic rigor[9] and accessibility" to secondary school subjects. A report based on teachers' views told how many senior staff believed subjects such as English, mathematics, science and geography were being squeezed out by "lifestyle" lessons.

---

1 mop up: erledigen, beenden
2 agenda: Programm, Tagesordnung
3 to encroach: eingreifen
4 to launch something: etwas einführen
5 to marginalize: an den Rand drängen
6 dissemination: Weitergabe
7 diluted: verwässert (hier im Sinne von: verringert)
8 to perpetuate: endlos fortsetzen
9 rigor: Strenge

Progress Check 3: EDUCATION & SOCIAL ISSUES

Under Labour, classes in personal, social, health and economic education (PSHE) have been introduced, covering subjects such as sex education, teenage pregnancy, alcohol and drug abuse, racism, bullying, managing finances and healthy eating. New-style lessons in citizenship have also been put on the National Curriculum.

But the report said: "The view was expressed that, in the past 20 years, there has been too much encroachment of politics into education, into areas which should be left to the professional judgement of the educators – as they are in many overseas countries – and that such lack of trust is dangerous. "It was felt that other countries give much more recognition to the educational role of teachers. By contrast, in this country schools are asked to do too many other things: to mop up all kinds of social problems, like obesity, that really aren't their business. By way of illustration, the 2004 policy document 'Every Child Matters' has 25 aims; only two of them deal with academic subjects." The comments come just weeks after the new coalition government axed[1] the Department for Children, Schools and Families in favor of the Department for Education. The move was seen as an attempt to re-focus the priorities of the Whitehall department back onto education. In recent years, John Dunford, general secretary of the Association of School and College Leaders, has criticized the extent to which schools have been forced to focus on social problems. He said that schools "can't and shouldn't replace the role of parents".

		T	F	Justification
0	Teachers spend less time on the academic side of teaching as they concentrate on other problems such as obesity.	✗		An over-emphasis on ...
Q13	"Every Child Matters" is a document offering educational guidelines only.			
Q14	According to Bernice McCabe, many teachers nowadays focus on educational agendas.			
Q15	McCabe believes that children nowadays do not have as much subject knowledge as they used to.			
Q16	The PTI owes its existence to a member of the Royal Family.			
Q17	PSHE does not focus on academic subjects such as maths and languages.			
Q18	It is reported that British teachers should focus more on real problems such as obesity and other kinds of social problems.			
Q19	Mr. Dunford is of the opinion that some educational responsibilities should stay within the families.			

7 points
(1 point each)

Question Time: "Schools forced to 'mop up social problems'"

Reflect on the text and answer the questions below.

- What kind of problems do many young people, according to the text, face nowadays?
- What do we learn about teachers and their training?
- What is your opinion on the "social rather than educational agenda" at school?

[1] to axe: rücksichtslos beseitigen

TIME FRAME
15 min

Listening Comprehension

CD-TRACK 03

You are going to hear a radio show on the importance of play for children.
You have 45 seconds to read the sentences below before the text will be played to you twice. While listening, match the beginnings of the sentences (Q1–Q8) with the sentence endings (A–K). Write your answers in the table provided. There are two extra sentence endings that do not belong to the text at all. We have done the first example (0) for you.
After you have listened to the text twice, you will have another 45 seconds to go through your answers again.

0	KaBOOM! wants every American child ...
Q1	After a hurricane had destroyed Bay St. Louis ...
Q2	Mr. Darell Hammond believes that ...
Q3	Many American children ...
Q4	Adults often do not look ...
Q5	In order to be successful later on, children nowadays are meant to ...
Q6	Play is ...
Q7	Children who do not have the opportunity to play ...
Q8	Children who play have fewer difficulties ...

A	... focus on school and work on their CVs from a very young age.
B	... play in disused, vacant buildings.
C	... play at home and on specially designed playgrounds.
D	... after their children.
E	... figuring out how the world works.
F	... to grow up close to a place to play.
G	... at life from the viewpoint of a child.
H	... the city was slowly rebuilt but not the playgrounds.
I	... children's work.
J	... playing is generally good for children as it helps them in many ways.
K	... are pretty much "unemployed".

0	Q1	Q2	Q3	Q4	Q5	Q6	Q7	Q8
F								

8 points
(1 point each)

TOTAL
POINTS

Writing

Write all three of the required texts (A, B and C).

A. Blog Post (250 words, +/-10%)

As part of a school project you are asked to write a blog post discussing the following quotation: *"Schools should teach children first and foremost social abilities."*

Write a blog post discussing the statement above. In your blog post you should:
- discuss challenges teenagers face in today's world
- suggest a split of responsibilities between schools and families
- explain how schools should prepare their students for a life after school

Write about 250 words. Don't forget to give your blog a title.

B. Blog Post (250 words, +/-10%)

Teachers and students of your school have come together and have initiated "2gether", a non-profit organization that wants to bring people of all generations together. They focus on story-telling as a means of learning from each other. Students' parents and grandparents, teachers, partners, relatives and friends now have the platform to meet and exchange thoughts and ideas.

Write an introductory blog post, introducing the new project.

Your blog post should:
- describe the actual news
- explain the people, stories, dates and other aspects related with the news
- discuss the purpose of the project

Write about 250 words. Don't forget to give your blog a title.

C. E-mail (250 words, +/-10%)

Your headmaster has decided to modernize your school's library, cafeteria, and some of the classrooms. Together with the statutory elected panel of teachers, parents and pupils[1], he has found sponsors for this project and decided to start with buying new furniture for the cafeteria and the library and new blackboards for some of the classrooms. As an end-of-school project he has asked you and your classmates to help him. Write an e-mail to coolchairs.com, an international provider of school and office space furniture asking about their products.

Your e-mail should
- describe your selection
- state numbers of pieces needed
- give all further necessary details

Write around 250 words.

---

[1] statutory elected panel of teachers, parents and pupils = SGA – Schulgemeinschaftsausschuss

Speaking

A. WORK IN PAIRS: Discuss the following quotations:

- What are the following quotations about?
- Do you agree with what is said?
- Use the quotations as a starting point for a discussion.

I like a teacher who gives you something to take home to think about besides homework.
(Edith Ann)

Education [...] has produced a vast population able to read but unable to distinguish what is worth reading.
(G. M. Trevelyan)

Education is what remains after one has forgotten everything one learned in school.
(Albert Einstein)

An educational system isn't worth a great deal if it teaches young people how to make a living but doesn't teach them how to make a life.
(Source Unknown)

In matters of truth and justice, there is no difference between large and small problems, for issues concerning the treatment of people are all the same.
(Albert Einstein)

To be social is to be forgiving.
(Robert Frost)

B. Describe the following images and answer the questions below:

1. What do you see?
2. Where and when – do you think – were photos 1, 2, and 3 taken?
3. What do you think will happen next in each of these situations?
4. How do you feel when looking at these images?
5. Who, in your opinion, took the photos/created the image?

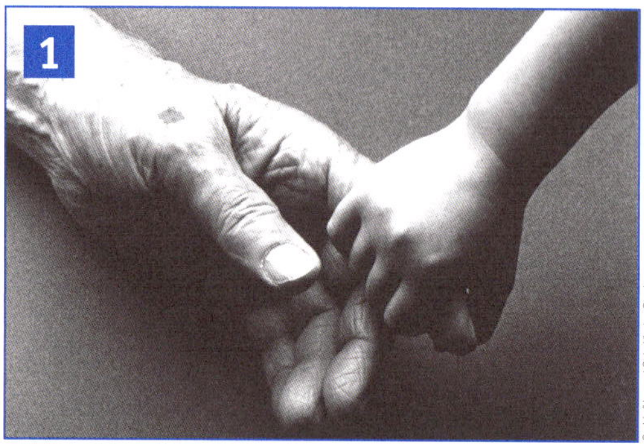

Corbis/Howard Sokol/Index Stock

www.neverforget.at

ingimage.com

Progress Check 4: MONEY RULES & BUSINESS MATTERS

TIME FRAME
20 min

Reading Comprehension 1

You are going to read an article about the invention of the automatic cash machine. Read the text carefully and decide for each sentence (Q1–Q7) which answer (A, B, C or D) is the correct one. Put an ✗ in the correct box. We have done the first example (0) for you.

John Shepard-Barron. Entrepreneur who invented the automatic cash machine and spared the world six-figure PINs

John Shepard-Barron, who has died aged 84, was credited[1] with inventing the world's first automatic cash machine, popularly known as the "hole in the wall" but more properly the automated teller machine (ATM).

Shepard-Barron once explained that he came up with the idea of cash dispensers[2] in 1965 while lying in his bath after finding his bank closed. It was then his habit to withdraw money[3] on a Saturday, but on this particular weekend he had arrived one minute late and found the bank doors locked against him. Later that year, he bumped into the chief general manager of Barclays Bank who was about to have lunch. Over a pink gin, Shepard-Barron asked him for 90 seconds to pitch[4] his idea for a cash machine.

"I told him I had an idea that if you put your standard Barclays cheque through a slot in the side of the bank, it would deliver standard amounts of money around the clock. He said, 'Come and see me on Monday morning'." Barclays commissioned[5] Shepard-Barron to build six cash dispensers, the first of which was installed at a branch in the north London suburb of Enfield on June 27 1967.

[...]

As part of his work in developing the self-service ATM, which would dispense banknotes 24 hours a day, seven days a week, Shepard-Barron also came up with the idea of a four-digit PIN, which subsequently transformed the way people across the world handle financial transactions.

Recalling his Army number, he had originally intended to make personal identification numbers (PINs) six digits long, but reduced the number to four when his wife, Caroline, complained that six was too many. "Over the kitchen table, she said she could only remember four figures, so because of her, four figures became the world standard", he recalled.

Shepard-Barron hit upon the notion[6] of an automated cash machine by thinking of the way chocolate dispensers worked. "It struck me there must be a way I could get my own money, anywhere in the world or the UK", he said in a BBC Radio interview in 2007. "I hit upon the idea of a chocolate bar dispenser but replacing chocolate with cash."

With plastic bank cards bearing magnetic strips still to be invented, Shepard-Barron's early machines used special cheques that were chemically coded by being impregnated with carbon-14, a mildly radioactive substance. Customers placed the cheque in a drawer, the machine detected the material and matched the cheque against a PIN before paying out a maximum of 10 pounds a time. "But that was regarded then as quite enough for a wild weekend", he noted. Asked about health fears, Shepard-Barron calculated that a user would have to eat 136 000 chemically-treated cheques to suffer any ill-effect.

According to the ATM Industry Association, there are now more than 1.7 million ATMs around the world. In Britain alone a total of 10 billion pounds a month was withdrawn from ATMs last year, with an average of a million transactions per hour.

---

[1] to be credited with something: etwas wird jemandem zugeschrieben
[2] cash dispenser: Bankomat
[3] to withdraw money: Geld abheben
[4] to pitch (coll.): anpreisen
[5] to commission somebody: jemanden beauftragen
[6] to hit upon the notion: auf die Idee kommen

0 John Shepard-Barron

A	invented the cash machine.	✗
B	was the first to use an ATM machine.	
C	was arrested for putting a hole in a wall.	
D	is still alive.	

Q1 In 1965

A	John Shepard-Barron usually picked up some money on a weekday.	
B	John Shepard-Barron usually picked up some money from the bank on the weekend.	
C	John Shepard-Barron always managed to withdraw money on Saturdays.	
D	John Shepard-Barron never withdrew money on the weekend.	

Q2 The chief general manager of Barclays Bank

A	had the idea of a slot machine that delivered money around the clock.	
B	ignored John Shepard-Barron's ideas completely.	
C	asked Mr. Shepard-Barron for 90 seconds of speaking time.	
D	was introduced to the idea of a machine that delivered money all day and all night.	

Q3 Barclays Bank asked Mr. Shepard-Barron

A	to show actor Reg Varney how to use the six new machines.	
B	to visit them at six to discuss the new machines.	
C	to develop cash machines for them.	
D	to build six money counting machines.	

Q4 Mr. Shepard-Barron also

A	introduced the pin code consisting of four numbers that changed the handling of money transactions around the world for the better.	
B	introduced the pin code consisting of four numbers that was long ignored as far as the handling of money transactions around the world was concerned.	
C	introduced the pin code consisting of four letters that changed the handling of money transactions around the world for the worse.	
D	introduced the pin code consisting of four letters that changed the handling of money transactions around the world for the better.	

Q5 Chocolate bar machines

A	were also invented by Mr. Shepard-Barron.	
B	were invented right after cash dispensers.	
C	existed before cash machines were invented.	
D	also dispensed money back then.	

Q6 The earliest cash machines worked with

A	plastic bank cards that had magnetic strips.	
B	plastic bank cards that had no magnetic strips yet.	
C	special cheque cards bearing magnetic strips.	
D	special cheques that had no magnetic strips.	

Q7 The early cash machines

A	harmed your health.	
B	were highly dangerous.	
C	allowed withdrawals of 1 billion pounds a month.	
D	paid out no more than 10 pounds each time.	

7 points
(1 point each)

Question Time: "John Shepard-Barron. Entrepreneur who invented the automatic cash machine and spared the world six-figure PINs"

Reflect on the text and answer the questions below.

- What do we learn about John Shepard-Barron?
- What does the text tell us about the development of the self-service ATM?
- Can you imagine a world without ATMs?

TIME FRAME
20 min

Reading Comprehension 2 ✓

You are going to read the article "Keeping it in the family". Read the text carefully and decide whether the statements (Q8–Q15) in the box below are true (T) or false (F). Mark the correct answer with an ✗. Furthermore, justify your answer by quoting the first 4 words of the sentence that gives away the answer (T or F) and write it in the column "Justification". We have done the first example (0) for you.

Keeping it in the family
By Heide B. Malhotra

Much of the world's economy is running on family-owned businesses – but many are not passed to the next generation. Worldwide, four-fifths of all businesses are family owned. In Europe, more than 75 per cent of all businesses are family owned, providing close to half of all available jobs. The majority of those businesses employ fewer than 10 people, according to a study by the KMU Austria Research Institute. In the United States, family-owned businesses account for roughly half of the country's GDP[1]. Such businesses could be a small mom-and-pop store[2] employing no more than two people, a medium-sized enterprise, or even a Fortune 500 corporation. [...]
With family businesses comes the all-important issue of succession: family feuds[3] or simply the lack of a suitable candidate within the family can cripple[4] a successful business when the time comes to hand over the reins[5]. Most don't make it to the second generation and only about one tenth stay in the family over 60 years.
Experts suggest that for a company to remain competitive, a company should strike out and consider hiring from outside the family, as it is not that often that a successor[6] who possesses all that is needed to head a business can be found within the family.
"It may make more sense – even if the successors to the company's founder are in control because they own enough shares[7] – for subsequent generations to choose an independent professional from outside the clan to take over, experts note: someone with broader vision and experience than any family member", according to a recent Knowledge@Wharton (KW) report. But some survive longer within the family. An extreme example is Kongo Gumi Co., Ltd of Japan, which was owned by the same family for 1400 years. It was recently sold to Takamatsu Corporation, a large construction company, in 2006. The sale in this instance was because the company ran into financial difficulties, but often the hand-over to an outsider is the final result of irreconcilable[8] feuding. [...] Family members of the Redstone entertainment family business dynasty – which holds the controlling interest in CBS Inc. and Viacom Inc. – have been suing[9] each other back and forth for money, power, and succession, although the family patriarch is still very much alive.
Liliane Bettencourt, whose father Eugene Schueller founded L'Oréal, is in a fierce court battle[10] with her daughter, who wants her declared mentally incompetent for giving a younger companion $ 1.37 billion over the past eight years."Experts stress that it is very important to prevent the succession process from becoming an isolated, traumatic episode. Officials must provide a more permanent role for the process. Experts say this requires learning from what has taken place in the past, yet not forgetting that each moment in time requires a somewhat different formula for success", KW researchers said. [...]

---

[1] GDP (gross domestic product): Bruttoinlandsprodukt
[2] mom-and-pop store: Familienbetrieb, Tante-Emma-Laden
[3] feud: Feindschaft, Kleinkrieg
[4] to cripple: lahmlegen, stillegen
[5] to hand over the reins: jemand anderem die Zügel übergeben
[6] successor: Nachfolgerin, Nachfolger
[7] shares: Anteile, Aktien
[8] irreconcilable: unüberbrückbar, unverträglich, unversöhnlich
[9] to sue: verklagen
[10] fierce court battle: wilder, erbitterter Rechtsstreit

	Statements	T	F	Justification
0	Most family owned businesses are run by the same family for many decades.		✗	Much of the world's …
Q8	One-fifth of all businesses are not family-owed.			
Q9	Usually less than a dozen people work for European family businesses.			
Q10	Small American businesses have no influence on the country's gross domestic product.			
Q11	Not many family businesses exist for more than a generation.			
Q12	Kongo Gumi Co. was in need of money and therefore sold the extremely old family business.			
Q13	The Redstone entertainment family business is run by a model example of a peaceful and successful family.			
Q14	Mrs. Bettencourt's daughter caringly worries about her mother's mental state.			
Q15	There is no simple rule to follow when it comes to handing over a family business.			

8 points
(1 point each)

TIME FRAME
15 min

Listening Comprehension ✓

CD-TRACK 04

You are going to hear a radio show on Curricula Vitae[1] (CVs).
You have 45 seconds to read the sentences below, before the text is played to you twice. While listening to the show, answer the questions (Q1–Q8) in a maximum of four words. We have done the first example (0) for you. After you have listened to the text twice, you will have another 45 seconds to go through your answers again.

Get your CV noticed
By Niki Chestworth

0	The radio show hosted by Ann Marie Rose is called ____.	**Business Matters**
Q1	Mr. Hamlet Clubb works as a ____.	
Q2	Nowadays it is not only people working in the recruitment[2] business that have a look through the many applications[3] they receive daily, but also ____.	
Q3	According to Mr. Logan, a successful application has to include ____.	
Q4	Ann Marie Rose quotes Rachel Paul by saying that a CV is often the ____.	
Q5	David Clubb believes that it is very important that candidates write their CVs carefully and in a considered manner in order to best promote their ____.	
Q6	Ann Marie Rose mentions another mistake applicants often make, namely sending out ____.	
Q7	We learn from Charles Logan that it is important to send ones CV together with ____.	
Q8	In Hamlet Clubb's opinion, it is important for candidates to match themselves to the ____.	

8 points
(1 point each)

TOTAL
POINTS

[1] CV (curriculum vitae): Lebenslauf
[2] recruitment: Personalbeschaffung
[3] application: Bewerbung

Writing

Write all three of the required texts (A, B and C).

A. E-mail (250 words, +/-10%)

A young and well-renowned company in your hometown is looking for summer interns. You will soon graduate from school and are highly interested in a summer job/internship. The job offered by the company sounds like your dream job. You have decided to send in an application.

In your e-mail you should:
- discuss your interest in this specific company/this specific job (make up your dream summer job!)
- share your strengths and weaknesses; your educational background
- describe your expectations

Write approximately 250 words.

B. Article (250 words, +/-10%)

You are asked by the editor of your school magazine "HIP!" to write an article about your dreams and professional goals now that you are so close to graduation. You happily agree to write the article. You also promise to include some thoughts about your scholastic career and how you hope it will help you to succeed in reaching your professional goals. Do not forget the headline!

In your article you should:
- describe education/training needed for your dream job; description of the job: pros and cons
- discuss working hours, working environment; hopes and fears
- present money matters and career opportunities

Write approximately 250 words. Structure your article and don't forget to give it a title.

C. Report (250 words, +/-10%)

Your teacher has asked you to do a class project on the labour market situation for young people in Europe. You have decided to hand in a report based on the information you have gained from studying the graph and the article on page 42.

In your report you should
- analyse the chart
- briefly summarize the text
- discuss the findings: name possible reasons and suggest solutions

Write approximately 250 words. Divide your report into sections. Don't forget the headings.

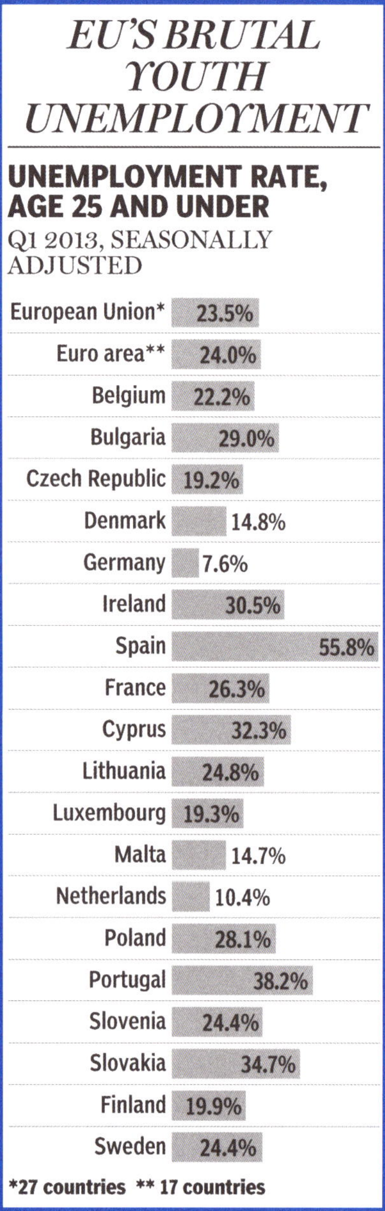

Germany warns of "revolution" as youth unemployment threatens to tear Europe apart

We need to be more successful in our fight against youth unemployment, otherwise we will lose the battle for Europe's unity

PARIS – German Finance Minister Wolfgang Schaeuble warned on Tuesday that failure to win the battle against youth unemployment could tear Europe apart, while abandoning the continent's welfare model in favour of tougher U.S. standards would cause "revolution". […]

"We have to rescue an entire generation of young people who are scared. We have the best-educated generation and we are putting them on hold. This is not acceptable", Italian Labour minister Enrico Giovannini said. […]

Germany in particular, weary of a backlash as many in crisis-hit European countries blame it for austerity, has over the past weeks taken steps to tackle unemployment, striking bilateral deals with Spain and Portugal.

German ministers told the conference that, to help young people find jobs, Europe must continue on the path of structural reforms to boost its competitiveness as well as make good use of available EU funds, including 6 billion euros that leaders have set aside for youth employment for 2014–20.

While all agreed on the urgency needed to tackle youth unemployment, ministers offered no concrete plans, insisting Europe must be pragmatic and work on various strands.

[…]

Speaking

A. WORK IN PAIRS: Discuss the following quotations:

- What are the following quotations about?
- Do you agree with what is said?
- Use the quotations as a starting point for a discussion.

I like to tell people that all of our products and business will go through three phases. There's vision, patience, and execution.
(Steve Ballmer)

A business has to be involving, it has to be fun, and it has to exercise your creative instincts.
(Richard Branson)

Family, religion, friends... these are the three demons you must slay if you wish to succeed in business.
(Monty Burns)

It is rare to find a business partner who is selfless. If you are lucky it happens once in a lifetime.
(Michael Eisner)

B. ROLE PLAY

This is a speaking task for a group of 3 candidates:
1 – the interlocutor, 2 – candidate A (John), 3 – candidate B (recruiting manager)

Interlocutor's Sheet: You, as the interlocutor, know everybody and all the situations. Make sure you follow the discussion carefully and ask about certain aspects if they are not mentioned by the candidates (see prompts).

This is what you tell the others at the beginning of the discussion:
John has applied for an interesting job and has been invited to an interview with the recruiting manager. John is well-prepared and eager to make a good impression.
Impulses are provided on your task sheet. They have to be discussed but you can also talk about other aspects.

These are the prompts for the other candidates:

PROMPTS FOR CANDIDATE A:
You are John. You applied for an interesting job and you really want to have it.

Discuss:
- your strengths
- your weaknesses
- why you are perfect for this job (be creative!)
- your educational background

PROMPTS FOR CANDIDATE B:

You are the recruiting manager of a well-known company. You are not sure about John's qualities but you want to give him the chance to present himself.

Discuss:

- John's strengths and weaknesses
- the job on offer and job requirements (be creative!)
- the company and its internal structure

Role-card for candidate A: Job interview

You are John. You applied for an interesting job and you really want to have it.

Discuss:

- your strengths
- your weaknesses
- why you are perfect for this job (be creative!)
- your educational background

Role-card for candidate B: Job interview

You are the recruiting manager of a well-known company. You are not sure about John's qualities but you want to give him the chance to present himself.

Discuss:

- John's strengths and weaknesses
- the job on offer and job requirements (be creative!)
- the company and its internal structure

Progress Check 5: SCIENCE & TECHNOLOGY IN THE LIMELIGHT

TIME FRAME
20 min

Reading Comprehension 1

You are going to read parts of an article from the Financial Times. Read the text carefully and answer the questions (Q1–Q6) by using a maximum of 4 words only. Write your answers in the space provided. We have done the first example (0) for you.

Charm, charisma and a sense of humour

By Haig Simonian

Within hours of his unexpected death on June 28, tributes to Nicolas Hayek came pouring in[1], as the man regarded as a farsighted entrepreneur[2] and face of an industry assumed his place in history.

Everyone drew attention to Mr. Hayek's faith in mechanical watch-making when others had written the sector off. And all praised his showmanship[3] and ebullience[4] as crucial factors in helping him to succeed in the hard [...] consumer goods business.

Now, almost three months later, it seems fitting to take a fresh and more distanced view of his achievements, enhanced by reflections from friends and counterparts. How deeply even fierce competitors[5] respected the 82-year-old entrepreneur emerged from the moving words of Johann Rupert, chairman and chief executive of Richemont, within hours of the announcement. "Nicolas Hayek's death is an immense loss for Switzerland and for the watch industry. He was the driving force behind Swiss watch-making, its leader and its saviour[6]. Our industry has lost one of its champions, respected by everyone who dealt with him; a man of honour and great charm", the tough Richemont boss wrote.

Today, after an emotional memorial ceremony in Bern Cathedral attended by hundreds of friends and followers, the comments remain fulsome. Jean-Claude Biver, head of Hublot and for more than 11 years an executive of Swatch Group and its predecessor[7], knew from his first meeting with Mr. Hayek on the sale of Blancpain in July 1992 that he was dealing with someone out of the ordinary. "After we signed the contract, he told me it was his habit to drink a glass of port to settle a deal and for good luck. So we did, at 11.20 in the morning! What impressed me above all was that he was always available – much more so than many middle managers. Seven days a week, twenty-four hours a day. He had this extraordinary ability to listen. He paid careful attention to what he was told, because he understood the importance of keeping in touch and having all the information at his fingertips."

Charm and charisma are the two personal qualities Mr. Biver remembers best. "Somewhat unusually among top bosses, who can often be dry or hard, he had great charm and a sense of humour. He could put people at their ease immediately. Even in difficult situations, he could relieve the tension."

But like most watch industry leaders, Mr. Biver devotes his warmest comments to Mr. Hayek's savvy[8] as an industrialist and entrepreneur. Few may now remember the minutiae[9] of the 1970s Swiss watch crisis, as first SSIH and then ASUAG – the two watch and component making conglomerates[10] of the time – wobbled[11] and then fell under the onslaught[12] of cheaper Asian quartz products.

---

[1] to pour in: hereinströmen
[2] farsighted entrepreneur: weitsichtiger Unternehmer
[3] showmanship: geschickte Zurschaustellung
[4] ebullience: Überschwänglichkeit
[5] fierce competitors: erbitterte Konkurrenten
[6] saviour: RetterIn
[7] predecessor: VorgängerIn
[8] savvy: Intelligenz, Klugheit, Grips
[9] minutiae: Einzelheiten, Details
[10] conglomerates: Großkonzerne
[11] to wobble: schwanken, wackeln
[12] onslaught: Angriff, Ansturm

In 1981, Mr. Hayek made his entrance. Already an established management consultant specialising in heavy industry, his Hayek Engineering group was called in by the two groups' creditor banks. In a series of what would be seminal reports about the prospects for survival, Hayek Engineering's studies between 1981 and 1983 recommended a merger[1], drastic cost-cutting and far greater emphasis on products and marketing.

Then, crucially, in January 1985, Mr. Hayek who was growing increasingly restless as a consultant and wanted to become an entrepreneur, bought an option on a majority stake[2]. The rest, as they say, is history.

But in the new English translation of a book about "Mr. Swatch" published last month, author Jürg Wegelin sheds light on crucial points in Mr. Hayek's career – including the fact that the investment was opposed by many of his closest advisers. The short book, which also devotes space to Mr. Hayek's seldom recorded early years in Lebanon and Switzerland, is marred[3] by some over-literal translations and assumptions about English speaking readers' knowledge of Swiss business, culture, and politics. But it provides useful detail on aspects of Mr. Hayek's life and career that Swatch Group has sometimes neglected. Although the book is broadly complimentary, it was not authorised, and, on initial publication in German, was viewed with suspicion by its subject and his group. Swatch prefers to direct inquirers to another – uncritical – work, based entirely on long conversations with Mr. Hayek.

A crucial chapter of the unauthorised biography involves clarification about the origin of the Swatch and the fact that this timekeeping breakthrough had been under development long before Mr. Hayek's arrival. Attributable largely to a pair of specialists under Ernst Thompke, the cheap, trendy and reliable Swatch was a vital contributor to the industry's renaissance. But it was neither invented nor even instigated[4] by Mr. Hayek.

"As an industrialist he was unbeatable", says Francoise-Paul Journe, one of Switzerland's most respected premium watchmakers. "But, one day, someone should write an authoritative biography that takes stock of the situation as it actually was. The arrival of the Swatch revived people's hopes in the industry. But don't forget, watches were still being made successfully in Switzerland." Even close allies[5], such as Mr. Biver, acknowledged the need for perspective, given the – perhaps inevitable[6] – concentration over the years on just one man. "Obviously, there were other brands: Rolex, Patek Philippe, Audemars, Piguit that contributed enormously to the prestige of Swiss watch-making," he acknowledges. But they didn't play the industrial role that Hayek achieved for his group. He revived an industry, not just a brand. An entire industrial fabric – that's the big difference."

The Swatch Group – a company prone to[7] hyperbole[8] when talking about its people or products, notes: "Mr. Nicholas G. Hayek's greatest merit was his enormous contribution to the saving of the Swiss watch industry and the foundation and the commercial development of the Swatch Group. Mr. Nicholas G. Hayek's extraordinary vision enabled him to realise and ensure the sustainability of a strong watchmaking enterprise with high Swiss added value. He is rightly recognized as a leading entrepreneur in this country."

---

1 merger: Firmenzusammenschluss
2 majority stake: Mehrheitsanteil
3 marred: geschädigt, ruiniert
4 instigated: angeregt, initiiert
5 allies: Verbündete
6 inevitable: notwendig, unvermeidlich
7 to be prone to: anfällig sein für
8 hyperbole: Übertreibung

0	Mr. Hayek always believed in ______.	**mechanical watch-making**
Q1	The chairman of Richemont also paid tribute to Mr. Hayek, even though they were ______.	
Q2	Mr. Hayek was a person who used to listen carefully to what others had to say as he knew how crucial it was to be informed and to ______.	
Q3	Besides Mr. Hayek's sense of humor, people like Mr. Beaver also appreciated his ______.	
Q4	As a consultant for the creditor banks of SSIH and ASUAG, Mr. Hayek gave the advice to merge the companies, to concentrate on marketing and products, and to ______.	
Q5	To understand the English translation of "Mr. Swatch" correctly, the English-speaking reader would have to know quite a bit about ______ in Switzerland.	
Q6	Switzerland knows that Mr. Hayek was one of its ______.	

6 points
(1 point each)

Question Time: "Charm, charisma and a sense of humour"

Reflect on the text and answer the questions below.

- Which of Mr. Hayek's character traits and personal qualities does the text talk about?
- What do we learn about the book "Mr. Swatch"?
- What does the text tell us about Swatch watches?

TIME FRAME
20 min

Reading Comprehension 2

You are going to read an article on Women in Science. However, some parts of the text are missing. Choose the correct answer (A–K) for each gap (Q7–Q14). There are two extra parts that do not belong to the article at all. Write your answers in the boxes below. We have done the first example (0) for you.

Women in Science See Risk and Reward
By Katrin Bennhold

The quiet revolution that has seen women (0) __________ with men in the work force and in education has also touched science, that most stubbornly male bastion.
Last year, three women (Q7) __________ prizes in the sciences – a record. Women now earn 42 percent of the science degrees in the 30 countries of the Organization for Economic Cooperation and Development; in the life sciences, such as biology and medicine, more than 6 out of 10 graduates are women.
Younger women, too, are sticking more with science after graduating. In the European Union, the number of women researchers is growing at a rate nearly twice that of their male counterparts.
[...]
But if progress has been dramatic since the two-time Nobel physicist Marie Curie was barred from France's science academy a century ago, it has been slower than in other parts of society – and much less uniform.
[...]
However, throughout the world, only a handful of women preside over a national science academy. Women have been awarded only 16 of the 540 Nobel prizes in science.
[...]
Women get more degrees and (Q8) __________ in industrialized countries. But they are still paid less and are more likely to work part time. Only 18 percent of tenured professors in the 27 countries of the European Union are women.
And the big money in science these days is (Q9) __________ – the fields with fewer women. With humanity poised[1] to tackle[2] pressing challenges – from climate change to complex illness to the fallout from the digital revolution – shortages of people with the right skills loom[3] in (Q10) __________. Therein lie both opportunity and risk for women: In the years to come, the people who master the science will change the world – and most likely command the big pay-checks.
[...]
But stereotypes run deep. Blanca Trevino is a (Q11) __________ and chief executive officer of Softtek, the largest private information technology service provider in Latin America. She recalls that the kindergarten teacher would call her to complain about her daughter. "The lady told me that my daughter was making up stories, saying that her mother had an office and an assistant", Ms. Trevino said. "The idea that this could be true (Q12) __________."

---

[1] poised: bereit
[2] to tackle: angehen, anpacken
[3] to loom: sich abzeichnen

Progress Check 5: SCIENCE & TECHNOLOGY IN THE LIMELIGHT

In the Philippines, Lourdes Cruz, a biochemist and L'Oréal-Unesco laureate for the Asia-Pacific region this year, has had a successful research career between the University of Utah and the Marine Science Institute in Quezon City. There (Q13) ____________, let alone children, she said.
[...]
By 2017, a shortfall of 200,000 engineers is expected in Germany, and in Britain more than half a million skilled workers will be needed to satisfy the demands[1] of the green energy, aerospace and transport industries. "Everything is (Q14) ____________ in science; now the pieces have to come together", said Ms. Dautresme at L'Oréal. "I believe this century will see a lot more women become leaders in science."

A	... received Nobel
B	... in computers and engineering
C	... Mexican computer scientist
D	... many countries
E	... had never time for a private life
F	... score higher grades than men
G	... did not occur to her
H	... a career with family
I	... in place for women to succeed
J	... was never time for marriage
K	... across the world catch up

8 points
(1 point each)

0	Q7	Q8	Q9	Q10	Q11	Q12	Q13	Q14
K								

[1] to satisfy a demand: den Bedarf decken

TIME FRAME
15 min

Listening Comprehension

CD-TRACK 05

You are going to listen to a radio show on artificial life. You have 45 seconds to read the sentences below, before the text is played to you twice.
While listening, decide for each sentence (Q1–Q5) which answer (A, B, C or D) is the correct one. Put an ✗ in the correct box. We have done the first example (0) for you. After you have listened to the text twice, you will have another 45 seconds to go through your answers again. Ready – steady – GO!

0 The radio show is hosted by

A	Karin McCarthy.	
B	Kathrin McCarthy.	✗
C	Karin McCortney.	
D	Kathrin McCortney.	

Q1 Dr. Craig Venter

A	is a biologist.	
B	is a physician.	
C	is a research assistant.	
D	is a genealogy scientist.	

Q2 Dr. Craig Venter's creation of "artificial life"

A	causes controversy in the scientific world.	
B	is admired by everybody in the scientific world.	
C	seems to only bring advantages.	
D	has long been hidden from the scientific world.	

Q3 Mycroplasma mycoides bacteria are

A	known to be bigger than other life forms.	
B	known to be the smallest free-living animals.	
C	known to be the smallest forms of life.	
D	known to be the biggest bacteria.	

Q4 The genetic code of the new blue-coloured bacterium contains

A	a watermark including personal information about Mr. Venter and his wife.	
B	a watermark that includes names of members of the project team.	
C	a watermark including e-mail addresses and a reference to hidden money.	
D	a watermark that includes water.	

Q5 Mr. Venter points out that his creation has had great impact on

A	the world of science only.	
B	the world of philosophy and science.	
C	the world, philosophically and technologically.	
D	the world as far as research and religion are concerned.	

5 points
(1 point each)

TOTAL
POINTS

Writing

Write all three of the required texts (A, B and C).

A. Article – Greetings from the Future (250 words, +/-10%)

SMART, an English youth magazine, is doing a series of articles on science & technology and is interested in students' attitudes towards the rapidly changing world of technology. You have decided to send in an article.

Write an article for SMART about the constant and rapid progress in the world of technology & science and compare the lives of people belonging to your parents' and grandparents' generations with the lives of young people today.
In your article you should:

- share general thoughts about science & technology now and then
- discuss transportation, communication, media etc. now and then
- explain advantages and disadvantages of today's world in this context

Write approximately 250 words. Structure your article and don't forget to give it a title.

B. Report (250 words, +/-10%)

Get started, an international organization interested in how teenagers make use of smartphones, has invited students to write reports on young people's habits with regard to the usage of this modern technological device.
You have decided to send in your report based on the results of a survey that you and your classmates have carried out.

In your report you should

- analyze the charts next page
- discuss some of the findings that you consider most interesting, while also considering possible advantages and disadvantages
- suggest guidelines with regard to parental control and control by teachers and school authorities

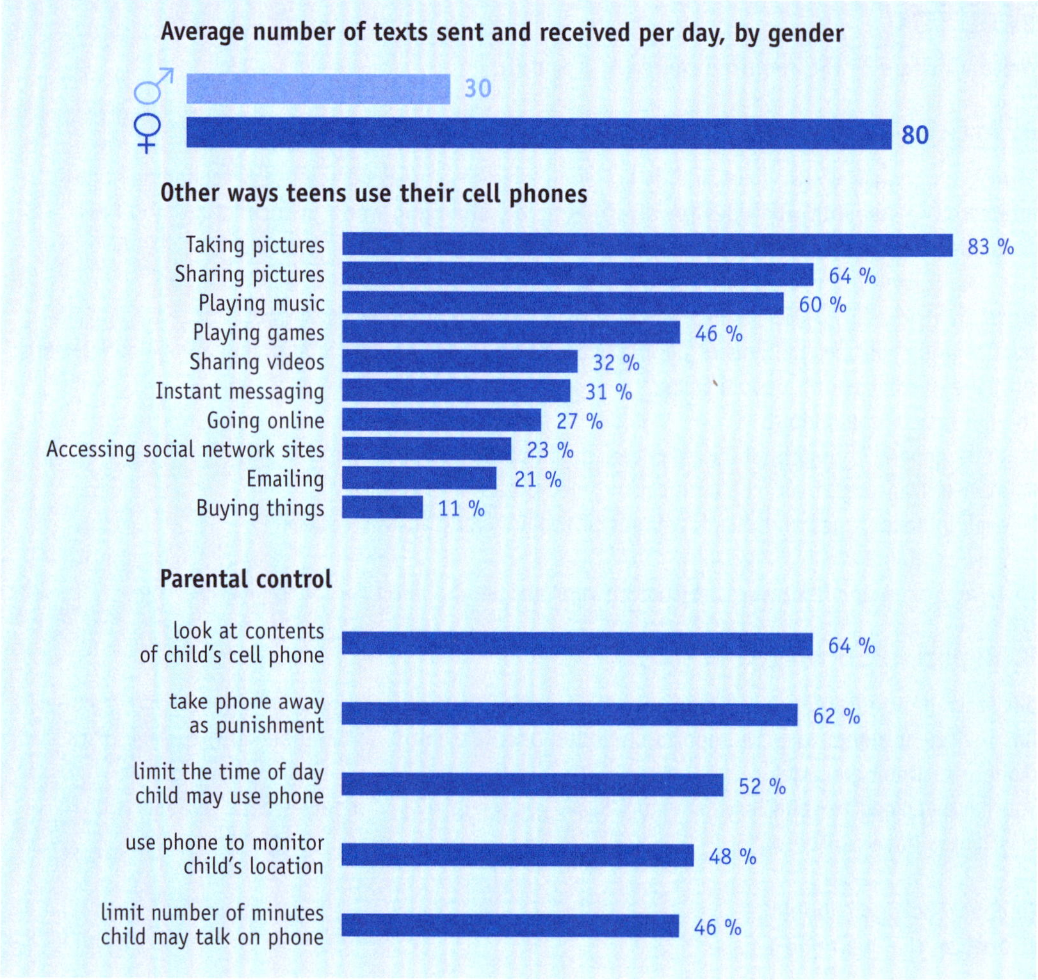

Write approximately 250 words. Divide your report into sections. Don't forget the headings.

C. Blog post (250 words, +/-10%)

As part of your school-leaving examination you are asked to plan and design a blog discussing the advantages and disadvantages of tablet computers in classrooms. Write an introductory blog post.

In your blog post you should:

- discuss possible advantages
- present some disadvantages
- suggest possible approaches to the introduction and usage of tablet computers in classrooms

Write about 250 words. Don't forget to give your blog post a title.

Speaking

A. WORK IN PAIRS: Discuss the following quotations:

- What are the following quotations about?
- Do you agree with what is said?
- Can you relate to them?
- Which one is your favourite and why?

All of the biggest technological inventions created by man – the airplane, the automobile, the computer – says little about his intelligence, but speaks volumes about his laziness.
(Mark Kennedy)

Modern technology
owes ecology
an apology
(Alan M. Eddison)

It has become appallingly obvious that our technology has exceeded our humanity.
(Albert Einstein)

The important thing in science is not so much to obtain new facts as to discover new ways of thinking about them.
(William Lawrence Bragg)

Science has made us gods even before we are worthy of being men.
(Jean Rostand)

B. WORK IN PAIRS: Have a look at the images below, answer the questions and use your thoughts as a starting point for further discussions with your conversation partner:

1. What is the thought behind the illustration? What does it aim to highlight?
2. What is shown exactly? How many items can you name correctly?
3. Try to match members of your family and ancestors with the illustrations. Who used what and when?
4. Now you: Which items have you used since you were a child?
5. Think of the future: Imagine the next illustrations. What would they look like? Describe the items in detail and discuss them with your partner.

TIME FRAME
20 min

Progress Check 6: HEALTH & NUTRITION

Reading Comprehension 1

You are going to read the article "Genetically Modified Fish Getting Closer To Tables". However, some parts of the text are missing. Choose the correct answer (A–K) for each gap (Q1–Q9). There is one extra part that does not belong to the article at all. Write your answers in the boxes below. We have done the first example (0) for you.

Genetically Modified Fish Getting Closer To Tables
By Andrew Pollack

The United Stated Food and Drug Administration (F.D.A.) is seriously considering whether to approve (0) ____________ that people would eat: salmon that can grow at twice the normal rate. [...]

The developer of the salmon has been trying to get approval for a decade. But the company now seems to have submitted most [...] of the data the F.D.A. needs to analyze (Q1) ____________, nutritionally equivalent to other salmon and safe for the environment, according to government and biotechnology industry officials. A public meeting to discuss the salmon may be (Q2) ____________.

Some consumers and environmental groups are likely to raise objections to approval. Even within the F.D.A., there has been a debate about whether the salmon should be labelled as genetically engineered (genetically engineered (Q3) ____________).

The salmon´s approval would help open a path for companies and academic scientists developing other genetically engineered animals, like cattle (Q4) ____________ or pigs that could supply healthier bacon. Next in line behind the salmon for possible approval would probably be the "enviropig", developed at a Canadian university, which has less phosphorus pollution in its manure[1].

The salmon was developed by (Q5) ____________ and would be raised in fish farms. It is an Atlantic salmon that contains a growth hormone gene from a Chinook salmon as well as a genetic on-switch from the ocean pout, a distant relative of the salmon.

Normally, salmons do not make growth hormone in cold weather. But the pout produces the hormone year round. The result is salmon that can grow to market size in 16 to 18 months instead of three years, though the company says the modified salmon will not end up any bigger than the conventional fish.

"You don´t get salmon the size of Hindenburg", said Ronald L. Stotish, the chief executive of AquaBounty. "You can get to those target weights in a shorter time." [...]

---

[1] manure: Dung, Mist

Mr. Stotish said the benefit (Q6) ____________ would be to help supply the world´s food needs using fewer resources. [...]

AquaBounty, which is based in Waltham, Massachusetts and publicity traded in London, said last month that the F.D.A. had signed off on five of the seven sets of data required to demonstrate that the fish was safe (Q7) ____________. [...]

"Perhaps in the next few months, we expect to see a final approval", Mr. Stotish said. He said it would take two or three years after approval for the salmon to reach supermarkets. [...]

(Q8) ____________ the drug evaluation process does not allow full assessment of the possible environmental impacts of genetically altered animals and also blocks public input. "There is no opportunity for anyone from the outside to see the data or criticize it", said Margaret Mellon, director of the food and environment program at the Union of Concerned Scientists. [...]

How consumers will react is not entirely clear. Some (Q9) ____________ that Americans are more wary[1] about genetically engineered animals than about the genetically engineered crops now used us a huge number of foods. But other polls suggest that many Americans would accept the animals if they offered environmental or nutritional benefits. [...]

A	... whether salmon are safe to eat
B	... for consumption and for the environment
C	... crops are not labelled
D	People at AquaBounty say ...
E	... the first genetically engineered animal
F	... public opinion surveys have shown
G	... resistant to mad cow disease
H	Critics say ...
I	... a company called AquaBounty Technologies
J	... held as early as this fall
K	... of the fast-growing salmon

9 points
(1 point each)

0	Q1	Q2	Q3	Q4	Q5	Q6	Q7	Q8	Q9
E									

[1] wary: wachsam, vorsichtig

TIME FRAME
20 min

Reading Comprehension 2

You are going to read the article "In High Schools, a Critical Lens on Food". Read the text carefully and decide whether the statements (Q10–Q20) in the boxes below are true (T) or false (F). Mark the correct answer with an ✘. Furthermore, justify your answer by quoting the first 4 words of the sentence that gives away the answer (T or F) and write it in the column "Justification". We have done the first example (0) for you.

In High Schools, a Critical Lens on Food

By Hannah Wallace

A commercial for McDonald's fish sandwiches played in a classroom at Park Slope Collegiate one day last month as part of a class called the Science of Food. It was clear that many students had seen the ad – several sang along with the jingle – but this was the first time they had been asked to critique it.

"Who is the target audience for this ad?" asked their teacher, Joni Tonda.

"Us!" yelled the 23 students, practically in unison.

Through the class, which is part of a new program being taught at 15 city high schools, students are becoming aware that they are part of a lucrative demographic, and they are learning how companies target them.

Media literacy is only one part of Ms. Tonda's lesson plan, which is based on a curriculum developed by a nonprofit group, *FoodFight*. The group's founders, Carolyn Cohen and Deborah Lewison-Grant, two former public school teachers, set out[1] to change the way adolescents think about food. By one estimate, 35 percent of adolescents in the United States are overweight or obese[2].

Though there have been several recent attempts to improve school food and to plant edible gardens at public schools – Michelle Obama's "Let's Move" campaign among them – those efforts have largely been focused on elementary and junior high schools.

"High school students have been ignored in this conversation about the obesity epidemic", Ms. Cohen said. "It's a serious health crisis."

The lesson plan blends[3] media literacy, politics, nutrition and cooking. Students learn how to evaluate food labels, to prepare nutritious and affordable meals, and to identify the political and economic forces that shape their diet. Some will visit urban farms, food co-ops and a 400-acre farm upstate.

Sarah Katz, one of the first teachers trained in the program, in August 2010, said the curriculum appealed to her because of its interdisciplinary nature and because it was not preachy[4].

"Telling kids what they should and shouldn't eat is not really effective", said Ms. Katz, who taught a class called Food for Thought at *Essex Street Academy* last spring. "Teenagers don't do things because adults tell them to. They need to care and have enough information to make their own choices."

A *FoodFight* course begins with a critical look at marketing campaigns. Some students react with outrage.

"Kids don't like to be played by corporations", Ms. Katz said. "They want to make their own choices."

---

[1] to set out: aufbrechen
[2] obese: fettleibig
[3] to blend: mischen
[4] preachy: moralisierend

At another point, the class discusses why some neighborhoods lack access to healthy, affordable food, an issue that resonates[1] with students because many *FoodFight* classes are taught in poor neighborhoods.
Students keep a food journal and learn how lobbyists try to influence federal[2] dietary recommendations[3].
In the lesson about advertising at Park Slope Collegiate, Ms. Tonda organized her students into small groups and asked them to create a slogan for a real or imagined food product. Three boys in the back of the class designed an energy bar called Pro-Fit. "It's more than protein; it's Pro-Fit!" their slogan read.
Takiyah Newton, a senior, said, "I signed up for the class because I wanted to learn about the food we eat, and society and stuff." A highlight, she said, was "learning about these companies and how they're tricking us".
Ms. Tonda said she had seen some changes in students' behavior. After a lesson about the consequences of consuming too much sugar, Ms. Newton switched from McDonald's sweetened iced tea to a no-calorie drink, Ms. Tonda said, and now brings bottled water to class. Another student, affected by the images of a crowded chicken farm in the documentary "Food Inc.", has asked her mother to stop buying meat from industrial producers.
Ms. Katz, at Essex Street Academy, was skeptical at first that her students would alter[4] their diets. But when she quizzed parents, it became clear that habits were changing. One student said he had cut out sugar-sweetened beverages. "His mom said, 'So that's why they're still sitting there in the fridge!' " Ms. Katz said.
Before Brandon Rosales took the class last year, he drank a lot of soda[5] and never thought about portion sizes. "I would skip breakfast, eat a light lunch and then stuff myself at dinner", said Mr. Rosales, who acknowledged that he was overweight.
After his food journal revealed the unhealthy pattern, he began replacing juice and soda with water, he said, and started eating smaller meals. Since he took the class, he said, he has lost 10 pounds, and he continues to maintain the journal.
"Now my food journal looks clean", he said. "My meals are good; I drink water. It's like a healthy person's journal." His family history provides some motivation. "I have a family full of diabetics", he said. "I want to live a happy life not having to put insulin in like my grandmas do."

Question Time: "In High Schools, a Critical Lens on Food"

Reflect on the text and answer the questions below.

- What is "Science of Food"?
- What do we learn about marketing campaigns in the field concerned?
- What do you think about "food journals"?

---

1 to resonate: seinen Nachhall finden
2 federal: bundesstaatlich
3 recommendation: Vorschlag, Empfehlung
4 to alter: abändern, modifizieren
5 soda: Limonade

Progress Check 6: HEALTH & NUTRITION

	Statements	T	F	Justification
0	Many students had already been in contact with the McDonald's ad before it was played to them by their teacher.	✘		It was clear that …
Q10	The class "Science of Food" is now taught in all American high schools.			
Q11	It is said that more than a third of all American teenagers weigh too much.			
Q12	Until now many projects on healthy food in schools have focused on younger children.			
Q13	"Science of Food" focuses on cooking only.			
Q14	Ms. Katz believes that in the context concerned adolescents have to be well-informed in order to be able to decide for themselves.			
Q15	In "Science of Food" lessons the question of availability of healthy food for everybody is raised as well.			
Q16	One of the students in Ms. Tonda's class especially likes acquiring knowledge about how her age group is played by companies.			
Q17	Generally these lessons do not seem to change the way students think and act.			
Q18	Ms. Katz learnt that her students still go for sugary drinks rather than healthier alternatives.			
Q19	Mr. Rosales has not learnt anything from keeping a food diary.			
Q20	Mr. Rosales' grandmothers suffer from diabetes.			

11 points
(1 point each)

TIME FRAME
15 min

Listening Comprehension

CD-TRACK 06

You are going to listen to parts of the radio show "Please Explain". You have 45 seconds to read the sentences below before the text will be played to you twice. While listening, choose the correct answer (A, B, C or D) for each question (Q1–Q8). Put an ✗ in the correct box. We have done the first example (0) for you. After you have listened to the text twice you will have another 45 seconds to go through your answers again.

Please Explain: Food, from the Farm to the Table

0 Susan Friedberg

A	... is a lecturer at Harvard University.	
B	... works at Dartmouth College.	✗
C	... studies at Harvard University.	
D	... studies at Dartmoor College.	

Q1 Leonard Lopate, the host of the radio show, wants to know

A	... whether there is a difference between American blueberries and blueberries from Europe.	
B	... whether there is a difference between local blueberries and blueberries that are shipped to America in winter.	
C	... whether blueberries from New York State are generally healthy or not.	
D	... whether many blueberries are shipped to America from Chile.	

Q2 Rich Pirog, associate director of the Leopold Center for Sustainable Agriculture,

A	... knows a lot about blueberries and talks about them in detail.	
B	... mentions that a South-American blueberry needs to travel quite a bit in order to reach the States.	
C	... compares the nutritional value of grapes with the nutritional value of blueberries.	
D	... loves grapes.	

Q3 Table grapes from California

A	... need about 2–3 days to reach Iowa.	
B	... are as good as those from Chile.	
C	... need about 17–18 days until they reach Iowa.	
D	... travel together with grapes from Chile to Iowa and the Midwest.	

Q4 Blueberries that can be found on American supermarket shelves

A	... before October are most probably imported ones.	
B	... are usually very cheap.	
C	... after October are most probably imported ones.	
D	... are rightly considered seasonal all year round.	

Q5 Susan Friedberg

A	... works in Burkina Faso.	
B	... has lived in Burkina Faso now for 19 years.	
C	... spent a few years in Burkina Faso.	
D	... has always worked in Burkina Faso.	

Q6 *Haricots verts* (green beans)

A	... are grown in France all year round.	
B	... are often imported from Burkina Faso.	
C	... are grown in greenhouses.	
D	... are very popular with African people.	

Q7 A few New York chefs

A	... use seasonal vegetables only because they consider it healthier.	
B	... don't use any seasonal fruit in winter time because of ecological factors.	
C	... use strawberries in winter time only.	
D	... never use raspberries or strawberries at all.	

Q8 The carbon footprint of food

A	... can be measured quite easily.	
B	... depends on various factors.	
C	... is measured in relation to airfreight as a means of food transport only.	
D	... is considered insignificant.	

8 points
(1 point each)

TOTAL POINTS

Writing

Write all three of the required texts (A, B and C).

A. Article (250 words, +/-10%)

Your teacher has asked you to write an article for this year's annual school report on your school canteen. The canteen was taken over by a new company a few months ago and has become famous for its junk food, sugary drinks and exorbitant prices.
First, have a look at the two menus below. One shows the offers of your old canteen, the other shows those of the new one.

In your article you should:
- describe the differences between the old and new canteen
- discuss the problems and challenges that come along with the new school canteen
- suggest further procedures for dealing with the situation

Write about 250 words. Do not forget to come up with a catchy headline.

OLD CANTEEN

Food served from 8 am – 6 pm

Food

Chicken Salad	2.50 €
Homemade Vegetable Soup	2.00 €
Multigrain Sandwiches	
Fillings: cheese, tomato, lettuce, beetroot, carrot, cucumber	1.70 €
Lunch Box: *wholegrain sandwich, bottled water, whole fresh fruit, cereal bar*	3 €
Fried Rice *(homemade, low fat)*	3 €
Corn on the Cob	0.70 €
Fresh Fruit *(seasonal)*	0.30 €

Drinks

Green Tea *(hot or cold)*	1 €
Milk and Soy Milk *(hot or cold)*	0.70 €
Tomato Juice	1 €
Orange Juice *(fresh)*	1.30 €
Apple-Carrot Juice *(fresh)*	1.30 €
Yogurt Drinks *(Strawberry, Mango, Passion Fruit)*	1.30 €
Water *(sparkling or still)*	0.50 €

NEW CANTEEN

Food served from 11 am - 2 pm

Food

Homemade Hamburger	6 €
Homemade Cheeseburger	7 €
Sandwiches	
Fillings: cheese, ham, bacon	4 €
Lunch Box: sandwich, Coke, chocolate bar	6 €
Hot Dog (with or without onions)	3 €
Noodles in a Pot	4 €
French Fries	3 €

Drinks

Soda (Coke, Fanta, Sprite)	2 €
Energy Drink	4 €
Milkshakes (Strawberry, Vanilla)	3 €
Cappuccino	2 €
Café Latte	3 €
Flavored Water	2 €

B. Blog Post (250 words, +/-10%)

A friend of yours has asked you to help him with his aunt's blog. His aunt has just opened the very first vegetarian restaurant in a small and very remote mountain village. With the blog she wants to present her restaurant to the locals who seem to be a little skeptical. Moreover, she wants her blog to attract people from all over the region and all she needs is an attention-grabbing text, describing the wonderful interior of the place, explaining the special menu and convincing everybody out there to come and try her lovely and healthy food.
Your friend has provided you with the information you need. Now it is up to you! Use your imagination and creativity and come up with a memorable text.

In your blog post you should:
- describe the interior of the restaurant
- discuss its cuisine
- outline the nutritional advantages of a vegetarian diet

Write about 250 words. Don't forget to give your blog post a title.

C. Report (250 words, +/-10%) ✓

Be healthy, an international organization that focuses on nutritional matters, has invited students to write reports on obesity and its impact on an individual's health.
You have decided to send in a report based on the graph on page 63.

In your report you should
- analyze the graph
- consider possible solutions and countermeasures
- explain your personal attitude on the topic concerned

Write approximately 250 words. Divide your report into sections. Don't forget the headings!

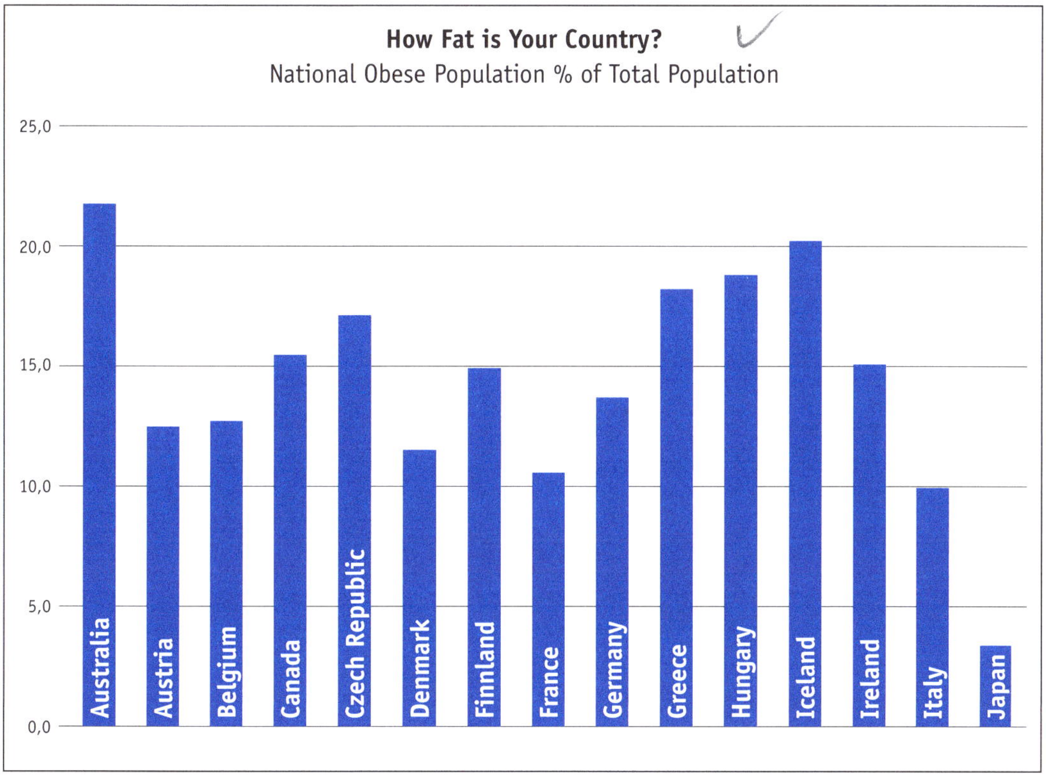

Speaking

A. WORK IN PAIRS: Discuss the following quotations:

- What are the following quotations about?
- Do you agree with what is said?
- Use the quotations as a starting point for a discussion!

I saw few die of hunger; of eating, a hundred thousand.
(Benjamin Franklin)

He that takes medicine and neglects diet, wastes the skill of the physician.
(Chinese Proverb)

The health of people is really the foundation upon which all their happiness and all their power as a state depend.
(Benjamin Disraeli)

I've been on a diet for two weeks and all I've lost is two weeks.
(Totie Fields)

I wasn't feeling well in the first half. I felt down, man. I had three slices of pizza before the game and the food took me down.
(Leroy Loggins, basketballer with the Brisbane Bullets, after 1986 semi-final)

What is food to one man may be fierce poison to others.
(Lucretius, 95–55 B. C.)

B. Individual Task

Have a look at the four photographs below. Compare and contrast them, and give your opinion about them. Imagine you are talking to a large audience that you are trying to impress. Watch your body language, gestures, mimics and language. You have three minutes. Try to keep talking and avoid any long gaps. Start by describing what you can actually see and then continue by comparing, contrasting, and interpreting.

ingimage.com

MEV Verlag/Susanne Holzmann

MEV Verlag/Micha Pawlitzki

ingimage.com

DEAR FUTURE VOCATIONAL SCHOOL GRADUATE!

As mentioned already, the following exams look exactly what your *Written Matura* (Reading Comprehension – Listening Comprehension sections) will look like.

Just for you to know:

Usually the general time frame of your written exam should look as follows:
1. reading comprehension tasks: 60 minutes
2. listening comprehension tasks: 40–45 minutes
3. writing tasks: 150–200 minutes

We suggest that you try to stay within this time frame while doing the test examinations.
Furthermore, it is important to know that each part (reading comprehension, listening comprehension and the two writing tasks) counts for 25% of the total exam and therefore also of your final grade.

Matura 1: Each "Q" is worth 1 point. Please correct Matura 1 according to the key provided and sum up all the points. To evaluate your achievement at Matura 1, please compare your results with the following table:

Points		Grade
from	to	
59	54	**1**
53	48	**2**
47	42	**3**
41	36	**4**
35	0	**5**

Matura 2: Each "Q" is worth 1 point. Please correct Matura 2 according to the key provided and sum up all the points. To evaluate your achievement at Matura 2, please compare your results with the following table:

Points		Grade
from	to	
62	57	**1**
56	51	**2**
50	44	**3**
43	37	**4**
36	0	**5**

Do not forget that the grade you calculated only makes up 75% of your total written Matura as the two writing tasks are worth another 25%.

All the very best!

TIME FRAME
60 min

MATURA 1

READING TEST

Instructions:

1. This test contains 4 tasks and 28 questions.
2. Write all your answers in this test book.

Task 1

You are going to read the article "Northern Exposure". However, some parts of the text are missing. Choose the correct answer (A–L) for each gap (Q1–Q9). There are two extra parts that do not belong to the article at all. Write your answers in the boxes below. We have done the first example (0) for you.

Northern Exposure
By Jennifer Davies

After 20 hours of traveling on three different planes, I was finally nearing my destination. From up in the air (0) __________ in the hundreds of miles of lakes and trees. I nearly missed Aklavik, which from the plane looked (Q1) __________. It was here in Aklavik, a remote village in the Canadian Arctic Circle, with its (Q2) __________ one grocery store and the snowy, bitter-cold wilderness as the only distraction, that I first became interested in medicine.

I had won a place on a gap-year program to help out at the local school. The village of Aklavik is surrounded by breathtaking beauty, but is plagued[1] (Q3) __________. As a teaching assistant, my job was to help out with everything from science to PE lessons, but in practice I (Q4) __________. I also offered one-to-one tutoring for students with special needs. Many are suffering from the effects of foetal alcohol syndrome (FAS), a big problem within the Inuit and Gwich'in community. Foetal alcohol syndrome is (Q5) __________ caused to babies when women drink during pregnancy. The high unemployment rate here leads many people to turn to alcohol and drugs, and their children are affected.

I tutored one girl who had the condition quite severely. At 13, (Q6) __________. I worked with her on practical skills such as cookery, finance skills and sewing. She was amazing. It was rewarding to watch her grow, but sad to see how something that could be prevented continued to affect people throughout their lives. During that year (Q7) __________ but also about myself. The town offered little entertainment, so we would read, play guitar and play board games. We went for walks. You only had to walk for five minutes and it felt like you were at the end of the world. The simple life is one of the best.

[1] to be plagued by something: von etwas geplagt werden

Since I didn't have the right A-levels[1] to apply for a medicine course, at the end of my gap year I applied to do a law degree. But something inside me knew it was the wrong move and I changed my mind. I went back (Q8) ____________, therefore opening the doors to a career in medicine. In Aklavik I learned to be more versatile[2] and resilient[3]. The small things don't bother me anymore (Q9) ____________ back to Aklavik and work as a doctor.

A	... home to Wales and spent a year doing a chemistry A-level
B	... by high levels of unemployment and by drug and alcohol abuse.
C	... she had a reading age of just six.
D	... because I know there are bigger problems. It's my dream to go
E	... I searched for any sign of civilization
F	... I keep looking for peace and quiet.
G	... found myself teaching.
H	... 350 inhabitants,
I	... I learned a lot about the community and their way of life,
J	... the name given to the physical and mental damage
K	... because I thought that they were small problems.
L	... the size of my thumbnail.

9 points
(1 point each)

0	Q1	Q2	Q3	Q4	Q5	Q6	Q7	Q8	Q9
E									

[1] A-levels: Schulabschlussprüfung
[2] versatile: vielseitig
[3] resilient: belastbar

Task 2

You are going to read the article "Oxbridge, red-brick, plate-glass or new-wave universities – why your college is not simply a set of buildings". Read the text carefully and decide whether the statements (Q10–Q16) in the boxes below are true (T) or or false (F). Mark the correct answer with an ✗. Furthermore, justify your answer by quoting the first 4 words of the sentence that gives away the answer (T or F) and write it in the column "Justification". We have done the first example (0) for you.

Oxbridge, red-brick, plate-glass or new-wave universities – why your college is not simply a set of buildings

By Hugh Pearman

When choosing a course, it is not just the quality of the teaching and the reputation of the university or college that matters – important though they are. Is the place itself agreeable, congenial[1], well connected – in other words, a place that you'd like to be? And which ones cut the mustard[2] architecturally?

Law schools fall into the same five broad categories as universities generally in this regard. There's the collegiate trio of Oxford, Cambridge and Durham (and King's College London, just pre-Victorian). Then came what used to be called the "red-bricks" or civic universities from Victorian times to the interwar years – Birmingham, Manchester, Liverpool and Leeds among them.

These were followed by the wave of architecturally ambitious "plate-glass" campus universities in the 1960s such as Sussex, the University of East Anglia, Warwick, Lancaster and so on; and finally there is the more recent wave of new universities, frequently the successors to former polytechnics, training colleges and other institutions, that came into being at the behest of[3] the John Major Government in 1992, and that were much encouraged by the new Labour Government from 1997.

As a consequence of this latest wave, many cities now have a number of competing universities, hence competing law schools. Mere newness does not necessarily mean shiny new buildings: some recent universities have taken over venerable[4], sometimes distinguished, stock.

The law course at the University of Greenwich, for instance – one of the newer crop of former polytechnics – takes place in the august surroundings of the former Royal Naval College by Sir Christopher Wren and others. And while the University of Durham is an early 19th century foundation, its oldest college is in the former Norman Castle, while its newest are outside the historic centre but still walkable.

Meanwhile, another of the older foundations, King's College London, is about to get older still, building-wise. It has always been sited right next to the Georgian splendour[5] of Somerset House, built from 1776 onwards as a place for civil servants. For some 180 years it has eyed up[6] its neighbour for expansion purposes. Now, King's has signed a lease to take over the East Wing, previously occupied by part of Revenue & Customs. The college's highly regarded 175 year old School of Law will move into the top two floors of this great building by the architect Sir William Chambers. In this way the college will break through the sublime courtyard of Somerset House and so be directly plugged into the cultural life of the capital.

---

[1] congenial: sympathisch
[2] to cut the mustard: es bringen
[3] at the behest of: auf Geheiß von
[4] venerable: ehrwürdig
[5] splendour: Pracht, Prunk
[6] to eye up: begutachten, mustern

MATURA 1

Some of the newer universities have resorted to supposedly iconic architecture to attract students. Examples with law schools include Salford and Northumbria (in Newcastle). Northumbria Law School is situated in a slightly alarming new £70 million campus of weirdly shaped buildings, set to the east of the city centre. But never mind: Newcastle is one of the great British cities, and the real stuff, including the popular regenerated[1] Quayside, is not far away. Salford similarly offers buildings that might be said to be a bit too showy – the Lady Hale Building, home of the new law school, has a rotunda equipped with coloured LEDs that glow at night. Well, so, what, really? But again, never mind. [...]

So my advice to prospective[2] law students anywhere in the UK-assuming your grades allow you the luxury of a certain amount of choice – is this. It is always about much more than your course and where you study it. Look at the complete picture of the cities your prospective law schools are based in or near. Are these places with a good feel that you'd like to visit and stay in anyway? If you can combine the pleasure of that with the best course you can manage academically, you're on your way.

	Statements	T	F	Justification
0	Only the quality of teaching matters with regards to choosing a university course.		✗	When choosing a course, ...
Q10	Leeds university was built long before the so-called Victorian time.			
Q11	Universities buildings featuring plate-glass came up in the Sixties.			
Q12	In many cities there are two or more law schools one can choose from.			
Q13	Architect Christopher Wren planned the historic building that now accommodates the law department of the University of Greenwich.			
Q14	King' College London is a fairly new school.			
Q15	King's College's Law School will soon be situated in the famous Somerset House.			
Q16	Parts of one building on the Salford campus are lit up at night.			

7 points
(1 point each)

[1] to regenerate: erneuern, umgestalten
[2] prospective: hoffnungsvoll

Task 3 ✓

You are going to read the article "Tiny Screens Bearing Tiny Delights". Read the text carefully. Then complete the sentences (Q17–Q22) on the next page by using a maximum of 4 words. Write your answers in the space provided. We have done the first example (0) for you.

Tiny Screens Bearing Tiny Delights

By David Pogue

Put Sifteo cubes in front of someone who's never seen them before, and you'll think somebody is reading the thesaurus[1]. "Cool!" "Neat!" "Awesome!" "Serendipitous!" That's because nobody's ever seen anything like them. [...] Sifteo tiles[2] ($150) are white plastic blocks, 1.5 inches square and about a half-inch tall. Each has a color screen on the top.

The breakthrough idea, dreamed up by a pair of M.I.T. students, has three parts. First, the cubes communicate with one another wirelessly; they know when they're next to one another, and which side is against which side. (They don't have to be touching; they can just be close.)

Second, they have very sensitive tilt[3] sensors. Third, the top screen is clickable.

These three simple ideas, in combination, permit a huge range of games. In one, you guide a cartoon critter[4] along a path by tipping his cube so that he slides onto the next one. In another, you unscramble words by sliding the tiles into the right order on the table. In another, you can click a screen to advance to the next game level.

In many games, you can get back to the main menu by flipping the cubes upside down and back up again. Sometimes you reset or shuffle a game by shaking the cubes in the air. It works. The communication between cubes, the animation and the gravity simulations (when you tilt cubes) are smooth and seamless, creating a perfect illusion.

The company asserts[5] that this is more than a new game paradigm. They say it's a healthy, essential cultural shift. It's a return, they tell us, to the simpler times when play meant manipulating things – blocks, checkers, Legos – with your fingers on a table; a return to the pleasures of interactive, face-to-face, tabletop game playing – a retreat from the iPod Touch syndrome where everybody's face is bent down toward a different, isolating screen. Sifteo may well be right about that. But its amazing little cubes must first mount three obstacles[6] that loom before it like the Pyramids.

First – and this is the big one – the cubes don't work without a computer nearby. In addition to three Sifteo cubes and a charger (which has slots for six cubes), the set comes with a tiny white transmitter nubbin[7] that you are supposed to insert into the USB jack of a Mac or PC.

Then you download a program called *SiftRunner*. *SiftRunner* lets you shop the online catalog of games, download them to your computer, read their instructions and transfer them to the cubes (wirelessly, courtesy of that transmitter).

---

[1] thesaurus: Lexikon, Synonymwörterbuch
[2] tile: Fliese, Platte
[3] tilt sensor: Schrägstellungskontrolle
[4] critter: kleines Haustier
[5] to assert: behaupten, beteuern
[6] obstacle: Hürde
[7] nubbin: Dichtleiste

Once you've sent the games from your computer to the cubes, which can take about a minute, you can click a Play button on your computer's screen. At this point, the computer supplies both the computing horsepower and the music and sound effects, which add a great deal to the experience. […]

The second huge obstacle is the price: $150 is awfully steep[1] for three cubes. […]

The third obstacle is, of course, building a game catalog. Without games, there's no game platform.

Only 13 games are available now. The company says that many more, including some from big-name game designers, are on the way. In demos, some of them look creative and fun. For example, you might stack the cubes on edge instead of keeping them flat on the table. […]

If the company can find a way to make the prices lower, the cubes more self-sufficient and the game catalog more varied, that will be a happy niche indeed.

0	Sifteo tiles look like ______.	**white plastic blocks**
Q17	Even cubes that are not touching each other know when they are next to each other and how they are aligned just by ______.	
Q18	In order to reset a game players might have to flip or ______.	
Q19	Sifteo reminds us of old-fashioned games as it is also about manually ______.	
Q20	Once the desired computer game has been sent to the cubes, a Play button will appear ______.	
Q21	Besides being too expensive and being dependent on a computer nearby, the inventors of Stifeo have to face the challenge of ______.	
Q22	At the moment Sifteo players can choose from ______.	

6 points
(1 point each)

[1] steep: *gesalzen*

Task 4

You are going to read an article about "It's Not U. It's Me :(". Read the text carefully and decide for each sentence (Q23–Q28) which answer (A, B, C or D) is the correct one. Put an ✗ in the correct box. We have done the first example (0) for you.

It's Not U. It's Me :(

By Benoit Denizet-Lewis

Late last month, 200 teenagers from Boston-area schools gathered to discuss the minutiae[1] of Facebook breakup etiquette. Should you delete pictures of your ex after splitting up? Is it O.K. to unfriend your last girlfriend if you can't stop looking at her profile? And is it ever ethically defensible to change your relationship status to single without first notifying the person whose heart you're crushing?

These pressing adolescent questions were talked about at a one-day conference on "healthy breakups" sponsored by the Boston Public Health Commission. "No one talks to young people about this aspect of relationships", Nicole Daley, one of the conference organizers, told me between breakout sessions as teenagers swarmed a nearby cotton-candy stand. "We're here to change that."

Minutes later, 15 high-school students on a sugar high convened[2] for a session on "creating online boundaries". The girls outnumbered the boys, and they didn't hesitate to gang up on a charming – and, until then, immensely well liked – 17-year-old named Roberto, who proclaimed[3] with a bit too much gusto that "racing to update your relationship status after a breakup" is a healthy behavior.

That was just one of a handful of scenarios the teenagers debated and placed into "healthy" or "unhealthy" categories: others included "posting mean/embarrassing statuses about your ex" (unhealthy) and "rushing into a new 'Facebook official' relationship" (understandable, but still not healthy).

"Roberto, you're really going to run all the way to your house after school to change your status?" a 16-year-old named Lazangie asked, shaking her head. She knows a thing or two about Facebook-related breakups: her last relationship ended, she said, because her ex-boyfriend couldn't handle her male friends posting niceties on her wall.

"When I'm done with a relationship, I'm not going to wait a day, an hour or even 10 minutes to update my status", Roberto told the group. "When it's over, it's over. I'm done with you."

"The key word here is 'racing'", another girl replied with all the condescension she could muster. "Is that really healthy? Breaking up shouldn't be a competition!"

The group's adult facilitator – who wore a blue "Face It, Don't Facebook It" pin, in a reference to the apparently troubling trend of young people breaking up with one another via social media – nodded in agreement and suggested that Roberto consider taking a "technology timeout" the next time he felt compelled to race home and publicly declare his singlehood. Roberto agreed to consider it.

Throughout the one-day meeting, organizers did their best to make the teenagers forget they were about to learn something. They were encouraged to freely use their cellphones ("We're not the kind of adults who tell you not to use them!" an organizer boasted during the day's opening session), and breakup-themed songs, like Kelly Clarkson's "Since U Been Gone", blasted from the main conference room's speakers. The pandering worked: I saw only one teen roll her eyes all day.

---

[1] minutiae: Details, Einzelheiten

[2] to convene: zusammenkommen

[3] to proclaim: öffentlich bekanntgeben

To help the youngsters envision what a healthy split might look like, pictures and videos of several celebrity couples who managed amicable[1] breakups were projected onto a big screen. Justin Timberlake and Cameron Diaz, for example, were heralded[2] as healthy because "they're still friends and were able to co-star in a movie together". Their parting was juxtaposed[3] with those of Kanye West and Amber Rose (West wrote a mean song about her) and Sammi and Ronnie from "Jersey Shore" (Sammi supposedly defriended Ronnie's friends on her Facebook page), who each exhibited the kind of "unhealthy" breakup behavior that the Boston Health Commission hopes Massachusetts young people will rise above.
In that pursuit, organizers encouraged the crowd to eschew[4] parting ways over text message or Facebook, the most common teen breakup methods. [...] Attendees were advised – with mixed results – to bravely confront the awkwardness of face-to-face breakups. When the facilitator in a session titled "Breakups 101" suggested that teenagers meet with "and come to an agreement or mutual understanding" with a soon-to-be ex, a skeptical 19-year-old nearly leapt out of her chair in protest. "So, you're telling me that you're crying at night, you're not sleeping, you're eating all this food to make you feel better, and you're supposed to just *come to an agreement*?"
That sounded like wishful thinking to at least one teenager, who insisted that dating in high school is for suckers. "Who needs the drama?" she said, adding that many peers choose friendships or casual [...] relationships over formal romantic ones. "I've got enough problems without some stupid boy breaking up with me on Facebook."

0 Two hundred teenagers got together

A	... to talk about their friends' relationships.	
B	... to discuss the general advantages of social networks like Facebook.	
C	... to share thoughts about how to behave online at the end of a relationship.	✗
D	... to talk about Boston and its schools.	

Q23 The lecture on creating online boundaries

A	... was attended by more girls than boys.	
B	... was held by Roberto.	
C	... was scheduled for 15 minutes only.	
D	... took place in an overcrowded lecture hall.	

Q24 Lazangie

A	... has a lot of admirers who keep asking her out.	
B	... was left by her jealous boyfriend.	
C	... has recently opened a Facebook account as well.	
D	... completely understood Roberto and his way to deal with things.	

---

1 amicable: einvernehmlich, freundschaftlich
2 to herald: etwas ankündigen
3 to juxtapose: nebeneinander stellen
4 to eschew: etwas meiden, etwas scheuen

Q25 Roberto

A	… wore a blue pin.	
B	… got advice from the person in charge of the session.	
C	… completely objected to the idea of a technology timeout.	
D	… ran out of the lecture hall and raced back home.	

Q26 The meeting

A	… was organized like a professional international conference.	
B	… was organized and hosted by adolescents.	
C	… was organized by youngster who brought their music and showed off their mobile devices.	
D	… was organized in a way teenagers could forget that they were actually lectured.	

Q27 Justin Timberlake

A	… has already been Cameron Diaz's boyfriend for a long time now.	
B	… is best friends with Kanye West.	
C	… produces videos for teenagers to help them with their relationships.	
D	… was Ms. Diaz's boyfriend.	

Q28 The facilitator of "Breakups 101"

A	… suggested to use modern technologies for amicable breakups.	
B	… suggested that teenagers meet with their soon-to-be-ex frequently before they consider breaking up.	
C	… believes that brave face-to-face talks can lead to amicable breakups.	
D	… said that in break up situations it was normal to cry at night, not to sleep and to eat far more than usually.	

6 points
(1 point each)

TIME FRAME
40 min

LISTENING TEST

Instructions:

1. This test contains 4 tasks and 31 questions.
2. Write all your answers in this test book.

Task 1

CD-TRACK 07

You are going to hear a report on a football academy. Listen carefully and then answer the questions (Q1–Q6) below by using a maximum of four words. Write your answers in the boxes below. We have done the first example (0) for you.

0	What's the name of the presenter of the radio show *London Today?*	**Sue Sanderson**
Q1	How old are the girls who take part in the trial run organized by the Hampstead Football Club?	
Q2	Who sold a 16-acre site to Diane Culligan?	
Q3	According to Diane Culligan, what do they want to achieve for those who have not played much yet by opening a football academy?	
Q4	Which chance do they want to give youngsters?	
Q5	How many teams between "under 11" and "under 13" took part in the first academy tournament?	
Q6	What's CCFSA's first aim with regard to the newly acquired fields?	

6 points
(1 point each)

Task 2

CD-TRACK 08

You are going to hear an interview with country singer Mr. Chesney.
You have 45 seconds to read the sentences below before the text will be played to you twice. While listening, match the beginnings of the sentences (Q7–Q15) with the sentence endings (A–L). Write your answers in the table provided. There are two extra sentence endings that do not belong to the text at all. We have done the first example (0) for you. After you have listened to the text twice, you will have another 45 seconds to go through your answers again.

0	At the moment Mr. Chesney …
Q7	With regard to tone and culture between his employees, Mr. Chesney aims for …
Q8	Mr. Chesney's crew guys are always …
Q9	The person who wins the so called *merch lottery* …
Q10	The check that was written by Mr. Chesney at the end of the year …
Q11	In order to thank all members of his team for their good work Mr. Chesney …
Q12	Mr. Chesney does not only sing but also …
Q13	It was football that taught Mr. Chesney …
Q14	In the beginning of his career Mr. Chesney did …
Q15	After talking to his manager Dale Morris …

A	… the first ones to get up and the last ones to go to bed.
B	… invites only the wives of his employees to join him on Virgin Island.
C	… gets 100% of the revenues from that night's merchandise sale.
D	… was divided by his crew.
E	… Mr. Chesney started to be more attentive to details.
F	… employs 150 people.
G	… that one has to work hard for success.
H	… invites everybody once a year to a 7 day holiday.
I	… respect between everybody.
J	… not make any money at all.
K	… takes care of the business.
L	… not dare investing money.

9 points
(1 point each)

0	Q7	Q8	Q9	Q10	Q11	Q12	Q13	Q14	Q15
F									

Task 3

CD-TRACK 09

**You are going to hear parts of an interview about African art.
You have 45 seconds to read the sentences below before the text will be played to you twice. While listening, match the beginnings of the sentences (Q16–Q24) with the sentence endings (A–L). Write your answers in the table provided. There are two extra sentence endings that do not belong to the text at all. We have done the first example (0) for you. After you have listened to the text twice, you will have another 45 seconds to go through your answers again.**

0	Modern artists at the turn of the 20th century …
Q16	In the 1980s Mr. Call …
Q17	Having seen the show "Primitivism in Modern Art" …
Q18	The French artist who put a cap and headphones on the African figure …
Q19	Mr. Call is …
Q20	Mr. Call's art is about taking American things …
Q21	The artist's many masks …
Q22	For the artist the process of making a mask includes finding an object …
Q23	In the process of the artist's work …
Q24	The exhibition is on view …

A	… for about 6 and a half months.
B	… an African-American artist.
C	… found inspiration in African Art.
D	… namely building blocks or cells.
E	… no music is involved.
F	… went to see "Primitivism in Modern Art".
G	… drums play an important role.
H	… inspired Mr. Call to use the aesthetics of African Art in his work.
I	… and changing their appearance so they look African.
J	… most probably wanted to westernize it.
K	… and multiplying it so that it eventually becomes like a building block.
L	… all look African.

9 points
(1 point each)

0	Q16	Q17	Q18	Q19	Q20	Q21	Q22	Q23	Q24
C									

Task 4

CD-TRACK 10

You are going to hear parts of an audio guide through one of London's districts.

You have 45 seconds to read the sentences below before the text will be played to you twice. While listening, choose the correct answer (A, B, C or D) for each question (Q25–Q31). Put an ✗ in the correct box. We have done the first example (0) for you. After you have listened to the text twice, you will have another 45 seconds to go through your answers again.

0 London is

A	... the Washington DC of Great Britain.	
B	... the New York City of England.	
C	... the Los Angeles of the British Isles.	
D	... the British Washington DC, New York City, and Los Angeles in one.	✗

Q25 Rick Steves

A	... walks his audience through the district of Westminster.	
B	... walks his audience through all of London.	
C	... walks his audience to Big Ben.	
D	... walks his audience straight to Trafalgar Square.	

Q26 The Westminster neighbourhood

A	... is historic.	
B	... is London's political centre.	
C	... is very modern and upbeat.	
D	... is not really contemporary.	

Q27 The Prime Ministers lives

A	... in the House of Parliament.	
B	... at No. 10 Parliament Street.	
C	... near the river Thames.	
D	... at No. 10 Downing Street.	

Q28 As a matter of fact

A	... Big Ben is a thirteen ton clock that can be seen from far away.	
B	... Big Ben is a famous building that many people visit every year.	
C	... Big Ben is a thirteen ton bell that cannot be seen from the outside.	
D	... Big Ben is a ten ton bell that cannot be seen from the outside.	

Q29 For about 500 years

A	... the Royals lived in the Palace of Westminster.	
B	... Westminster Palace accommodated the London Police.	
C	... Kings and Queens were buried in Westminster Palace.	
D	... Westminster Palace was open to common people.	

Q30 In 1834

A	... a fire destroyed all of Westminster Palace.	
B	... a fire destroyed nearly all of Westminster Palace.	
C	... a fire nearly broke out in Westminster Palace.	
D	... a fire destroyed nearly all of London.	

Q31 The London observation wheel

A	... is a ferris wheel in a shape that reminds visitors of a bicycle.	
B	... is made up of 38 capsules.	
C	... is called the London Eye because of its shape.	
D	... allows visitors a great view over the city – on clear days, which are rare, especially.	

7 points
(1 point each)

ingimage.com

TOTAL POINTS

TIME FRAME
60 min

MATURA 2

READING TEST

Instructions:

1. This test contains 4 tasks and 28 questions.
2. Write all your answers in this test book.

Task 1

You are going to read the article "Hip-Hop, Folk and Karate Through a Strainer on a Hot Afternoon". Read the text carefully. Then complete the sentences (Q1–Q6) by using a maximum of 4 words. Write your answers in the spaces provided. We have done the first example (0) for you.

Hip-Hop, Folk and Karate Through a Strainer on a Hot Afternoon
By Gia Kourlas

What is there to do when a dance festival turns into an endurance test[1]? When biting flies become so aggressive that your legs feel as if they have caught on fire? Clearly, opening day of the Downtown Dance Festival – three hours, no intermission – was a tester.

On Saturday afternoon Battery Dance Company presented the first day of its summer event, now in its 30th year. While the program took place on a small white makeshift stage at the Battery Park lawn – it's a pretty, intimate spot shaded by a canopy of trees – additional programs will be held at 1 New York Plaza and at Dance New Amsterdam.

Hosted by Jonathan Hollander, the artistic director of Battery Dance Company, the show featured six groups, including Silesian Dance Theater from Poland. That company, directed by Jacek Luminski, had arrived only the night before; understandably, in "Formosa Olivares (Near the top of a mountain one can't get lost)", there were some signs of fatigue. The work began with four men playing with a ball – and tossing their bodies onto one another – before being joined by three women.

The folk-dance feel and the deceptively casual atmosphere were appealing[2] in this imaginatively named premiere; it stuck out, at least, from most of the other blandly traditional offerings. But when the dancers turned into runway models (here the music accidentally dropped out), then returned to their initial playfulness, the loose logic slipped away: "Formosa Olivares" became as choppy[3] as the Hudson River.

Lydia Johnson Dance offered excerpts of "Zero Hours", which transported six dancers to a harmonious world in which deliberate formations and pretty poses created an inoffensive whole. Ballets With a Twist, led by Marilyn Klaus, took a different approach to classical dance with two works from "Cocktail Hour", a suite of dances inspired by drinks. In "Absinthe (Prelude)" and "White Russian", the dancers mirrored their liquids – a green fairy with a candle in the first, and creamy gowns and tiaras in the second – but their technique was spotty[4], their point shoes dirty, and the fantasy of the numbers was watered down, especially in broad daylight.

---

[1] endurance test: Belastungsprobe
[2] appealing: ansprechend, reizvoll
[3] choppy: böig, wechselhaft
[4] spotty: unregelmäßig, fleckig, nicht einwandfrei

In "XIII," Murray Spalding Mandalas – a group of seven women in long dresses in tones of red – presented themes from 12 previous works by Ms. Spalding, who died in November. The dancers, including the regal Sharyn Korey, knit a web of intersecting lines rendering[1] the affect more joyful than dry.
Dancewave Company, directed by Diane Jacobowitz, presented high school students in works by Jawole Willa Jo Zollar ("Flashback/Flash Forward", a witty homage to funk) and Andrea Miller ("I Can See Myself in Your Pupil"). Even though Ms. Miller's work, at its core, remained tediously unoriginal, the dancers added an appealing zest[2] to the long afternoon, especially Sarah Beranbaum and Luis Angel Grande.
Balam Dance Theater, performing three works, definitely overstayed its welcome: here Balinese dance met modern dance, ballet and karate to create a wince[3]-inducing fusion. The group returned with "Folia-Visiones del Antiguo España", an awkward blend of Baroque and Spanish folk dance and bullfighting movement. Where was Ballet With a Twist when you needed it? A summer cocktail was long overdue.

0	The 30th Downtown Dance Festival was presented by ________.	**the Battery Dance Company**
Q1	The three venues are Dance New Amsterdam, Battery Park Lawn and ________.	
Q2	During the dance performance "Formosa Olivares", four men were ________.	
Q3	When the dancers of "Formosa Olivares" turned into models, ________.	
Q4	Marilyn Klaus' team presented "Absinthe" and "White Russian", two dances from "Cocktail Hour", a ________.	
Q5	The female dancers of Ms. Spalding's works were dressed in ________.	
Q6	The Balam Dance Theater presented a dance that combined elements from modern dance, ________.	

6 points
(1 point each)

[1] to render: ausführen, erbringen
[2] zest: Vergnügen
[3] wince: Zucken

Task 2

You are going to read parts of the article "As Networks Speed Up, Data Hits a Wall". Read the text carefully and decide whether the statements (Q7–Q13) in the boxes below are true (T) or false (F). Mark the correct answer with an ✘. Furthermore, justify your answer by quoting the first 4 words of the sentence that gives away the answer (T or F) and write it in the column "Justification". We have done the first example (0) for you.

As Networks Speed Up, Data Hits a Wall

By Jenna Wortham

The newest smartphones are intended to run on speedy 4G networks that allow people to effortlessly stream music, watch Netflix movies and tune in live to a Mets game, wherever they are. But there's a catch[1], of course.

Cellphone plans[2] that let people gobble up[3] data as if they were at an all-you-can eat buffet are disappearing, just as a new crop of data-gobbling Internet services from Netflix, Spotify, Amazon, Apple and the like are hitting the market or catching on with wide audiences. These services use far more data than simply checking e-mail or browsing the Web, so their heaviest users may find themselves running over their plan's monthly allotment[4] and paying extra.

The wireless carriers[5] say their tighter limits will affect only a small percentage of customers. And they say they are simply trying to get ahead of an exploding appetite for data and avoid problems with overburdened networks.

Mark Siegel, a spokesman for AT&T*, said that if current trends continued, the company's network would carry more data in the first two months of 2015 than in all of 2010. He described the pricing issue as a "balancing act", adding: "The tiered[6] data plans will meet the needs of the overwhelming majority of consumers. A lot of people think they're heavy users, but they're not."

But analysts say that inevitably more people will find themselves in the "heavy user" category, particularly as more of them trade in[7] their lower-end phones for smartphones and move to 4G networks.

For most people who use their phones to check e-mail, surf the Web and watch an occasional video, the move toward tiered pricing will not immediately raise their phone bills. Verizon's* monthly plan offering two gigabytes of data for $30, costs the same as its old unlimited plan, for example. But even now it doesn't take much for a media-hungry smartphone user to chew through two gigabytes; watching Netflix video for more than roughly 20 minutes a day will do the trick. And an extra gigabyte will cost Verizon customers an additional $10.

"Over time, as you give people faster devices with faster speeds, it's going to be a lot easier to hit that two-gig mark", said Philip Cusick, an analyst with JPMorgan Chase who follows the telecommunications industry.

In addition to worrying about overtaxing their networks, wireless carriers are looking for new ways to make money from mobile data and applications, rather than voice minutes. Over the last three years, the amount of money consumers spent a month on mobile calling declined to $30 from $40, according to Recon Analytics. During the same period the average amount spent on data nearly doubled, jumping to $13 from $7.

---

[1] a catch: ein Haken
[2] cellphone plan: Telefontarif
[3] to gobble up: verschlingen
[4] allotment: Kontingent
[5] carrier: Betreiber
[6] tiered: gestuft
[7] to trade in: eintauschen

* US-amerikanische Telefonbetreiber

"We've fallen in love with data and the utility that we get from it", said Roger Entner, an analyst at Recon. "The usage pattern has changed dramatically."

AT&T and Verizon have both phased out their unlimited data plans in favor of tiered plans. Verizon offers 75-megabyte plans for basic phones, as well as two-, five- and 10-gigabyte plans for smartphones, topping out at $80 a month. Those in the more expensive plans who go over their limit are charged $10 for another gigabyte, as are AT&T customers who exceed the limit on that company's two-gigabyte plan, which costs $25.

T-Mobile*, which AT&T is hoping to acquire, offers tiers from 200 megabytes up to 10 gigabytes. Those on the 200-megabyte plan are charged 10 cents for an extra megabyte. And if those with the upper-tier plans exceed their limits, the company slows their data connections until the next billing period.

Sprint* is the last carrier to hold onto its unlimited data plan, but analysts and industry experts say it is unlikely to last. [...]

	Statements	T	F	Justification
0	With the help of the newest smartphones, people can even watch sports games live.	✘		The newest smartphones are ...
Q7	Nowadays, more and more cellphone carriers start offering unlimited plans.			
Q8	By introducing tighter limits, wireless carriers try to deal with the challenge of overstrained networks.			
Q9	If trends at At&T didn't change, the amount of data carried by the network would grow sufficiently.			
Q10	The move towards tiered pricing will subsequently lead to higher phone bills.			
Q11	At the moment, it is nearly impossible to use up 2 gigabytes a month with a smartphone.			
Q12	People have always used their mobile devices in the same way they use it now.			
Q13	Customers of T-Mobile are offered tiered plans.			

7 points
(1 point each)

Task 3

You are going to read the article "For a Standout College Essay, Applicants Fill Their Summer". However, some parts of the text are missing. Choose the correct answer (A–K) for each gap (Q14–Q22). There is one extra part that does not belong to the article at all. Write your answers in the boxes below. We have done the first example (0) for you.

For a Standout College Essay, Applicants Fill Their Summers
By Jenny Anderson

Josh Isackson, an 18-year-old graduate of Tenafly High School in New Jersey, spent the summer after his sophomore year studying Mandarin in Nanjing, China. The next year he was an (0) ____________ in Shanghai. When it came time to write a personal statement for his college applications, those summers offered a lot of inspiration.

"When I was thinking about the essay, I realized that taking Chinese was a big part of me", he said.

So Mr. Isackson wrote about exploring the ancient tombs of the Ming dynasty in the Purple Mountain region of Nanjing, "trading jokes with long-dead Ming Emperors, stringing my string hammock[1] between two plum trees and calmly sipping fresh green tea while (Q14) ____________ on the horizon".

Jill Tipograph, who founded a consulting company called *Everything Summer,* helped Mr. Isackson plan the China trips. To Ms. Tipograph, his experience was the best possible outcome: he loved China, and the trips offered priceless fodder[2] for the cutthroat[3] college application process. (Mr. Isackson (Q15) ____________ Yale University this fall.)

"Students are planning their summer experiences to augment[4] who they are and discover who they are, and that absolutely helps the college process", she said.

Students (Q16) ____________ to college are increasingly tailoring their summer plans with the goal of creating a standout personal statement – 250 words or more – for the Common Application in which to describe "a significant experience, achievement, risk you have taken or ethical dilemma you have faced and (Q17) ____________". Specialized, exotic and sometimes costly activities, they hope, will polish[5] a skill, cultivate an interest and put them in the spotlight in a crowded field of straight-A students with strong test scores, community service hours and plenty (Q18) ____________.

A dizzying array[6] of summer programs have cropped up to feed the growing anxiety that summer must be used constructively. Students can study health care in Rwanda, veterinary medicine in the Caribbean or cell cloning at Brown University, or learn about Sikkim, India's only Buddhist state. For those who lack the means to pay for an essay-inspiring trip, at least (Q19) ____________ exists to help. […]

"The reality is that the whole process of getting into school is extremely competitive, and it's not only what you do during the school year – your grades and extra-curriculars", Mr. Isackson's mother, Marla Isackson, said. "It's your whole package, including what you do in the summer."

---

1 hammock: Hängematte
2 fodder: Futter
3 cutthroat: halsabschneiderisch
4 to augment: erweitern, vergrößern
5 to polish: polieren, den letzten Schliff geben
6 array: Anzahl, Reihe

Students do not have to (Q20) ______________ an essay-worthy experience. When Mary Lang Gill was a rising senior at the Atlanta Girls School, a private school, she hired Pam Proctor, an independent college counselor and the author of "The College Hook", a college admissions guide. After learning that Ms. Gill loved to paint, Ms. Proctor connected her to the Florida Highwaymen, a band of renegade[1] painters active during the 1950s and '60s.

"I spent a whole day with them", painting and observing, said Ms. Gill, who (Q21) ______________ College. "It was one of the coolest things ever, and I love that and I got to put it on my application." Ms. Proctor said she spent a great deal of time with students helping them find the right topic for the college essay. "Picking the essays is as important as writing them," she said. After that, she said, the stories "write themselves".

As colleges look for specialization, "mastery" and "passion" have become buzzwords at many New York City private schools. Along with the perception that perfectly developed essays are essential is the sense among some parents and teachers that colleges have shifted from valuing balanced students who excel in several areas, like history and ice hockey, to demanding students who (Q22) ______________________________ and have an area of "mastery", like squash or fencing, that showcases one's depth.

A	… one scholarship program
B	… will attend
C	… spend a summer abroad for
D	… preparing to apply
E	… intern at a market research firm
F	… of extracurricular activities
G	… perform well across all subjects
H	… watching the sun set
I	… its impact on you
J	… spend a summer abroad at
K	… just graduated from Dickinson

9 points
(1 point each)

0	Q14	Q15	Q16	Q17	Q18	Q19	Q20	Q21	Q22
E									

[1] renegade: abtrünnig

Task 4

You are going to read a Newsweek article. Read the text carefully and decide for each sentence (Q23–Q28) which answer (A, B, C or D) is the correct one. Put an ✗ in the correct box. We have done the first example (0) for you.

Nuts about Brazil
By Rob Smith

On the rare occasions when I'm fortunate enough to feast my eyes on one of the world's natural wonders, it has always been a humbling experience – a moment to reflect on life and my existence on this amazing planet. This time, though, it was more personal. As I, Rob Smith, cast my eyes around the breathtaking panorama – almost familiar from TV screens – there was another emotion sneaking up, one of nervous apprehension about what I'd been planning to do for months in this city.

I was looking down on the vast, natural harbour of Rio de Janeiro from Corcovado, the seven-hundred-metre peak towering above the city and the site of the famous Christ the Redeemer statue. This iconic statue of Christ, with its instantly recognisable, outstretched arms, was completed in 1931.

Facing the equally iconic Sugarloaf Mountain, it stands guard over this beautiful city and has become one of the world's most famous and photographed landmarks. From this elevated position you get a panoramic view of one of the most stunning natural landscapes to be found on any continent. And once you've taken the obligatory pictures of the statue – which on a clear day is worth the trip by taxi or on the cog train in itself – you still have the radiant vastness of Rio stretched out below you, as you plan your day.

Football fans will want to know that the home stadium of the most charismatic national football team in the world lies just behind the peak to the north. Opened for the 1950 World Cup, the 96 000 capacity Maracanã Stadium is almost a pilgrimage[1] site for some fans, and a tour round the ground that is to many the beating heart of world football – where the likes of Pelé and Zico scored their finest goals – just cannot be missed. Even if you don't manage to catch a game while you're here, you can still feel the passion, colour and relentless[2] samba drumbeat inside the stadium of a country that lives for football.

Copacabana beach, eastern most of the two sandy crescents fronting the ocean to the south, is perhaps the world's most famous seashore. On sunny afternoons, and at weekends, it seems as if everyone in Rio, from the poorest *favela slum-dweller*[3], to the richest mansion-owner, comes out here to socialise – to work on tans and muscle tone, display bikinis and shorts, and show off sporting skills. If you're lucky you may even get to see some of Brazil's sporting stars playing barefoot beach volleyball or soccer with the locals. […]

It was only a few weeks before Carnival and the samba school rehearsals were in full swing. At every turn we encountered hundreds of people giving it their all in preparation for the months of pure hedonism and spectacle that was about to hit Rio and the whole of Brazil. How could anybody not love a country where most of its inhabitants spend 11 months of the year, in ridiculously hot sweaty conditions, practising for the biggest month-long party in the world, only to start practising again as soon as it's finished.

---

1 pilgrimage: Pilgerfahrt
2 relentless: unbarmherzig, unerbittlich
3 slum-dweller: Slumbewohner

The vibe was fantastic, but it was the sight of Pão de Açscar (the Sugarloaf) that really made my heart beat faster. This peak of granite and quartz, rising nearly four hundred metres out of the Atlantic, is named after its resemblance to a block or refined loaf sugar. Every bit as symbolic of Rio as the Corcovado, a cable-car ride up to the peak of the Sugarloaf is an absolute must-do, and towards sunset, that's exactly where we found ourselves. Each cable car takes around 75 people and you get thrilling aerial views of the city on the way up, slightly dampened[1] in my case by increasing nerves about what lay ahead. Sunset is by far the best time to go to the Sugarloaf, as you avoid the crowds and get to see the sun setting directly behind the Christ statue on Corcovado as the city mutates from glittering daylight to steamy darkness.

I knew it was going to be perfect and, as I sat with Jo – the perfect sunset, as planned, in the background, – I swallowed extreme nerves and asked her if she would marry me. She said yes. Like the perfect Rio sunset, I was pretty sure it would work out.

0 Whenever Rob Smith had the chance to consciously experience the beauty of the planet

A	... he reflected on life.	✗
B	... he was reminded of TV shows and documentaries.	
C	... he feasted his eyes on everything around him for hours.	
D	... he thanked God for his existence.	

Q23 The famous Christ the Redeemer Statue

A	... is situated in the harbour area in Rio.	
B	... is situated in the natural harbour area.	
C	... is seven-hundred metres tall.	
D	... is situated on top of mountain Corcovado.	

Q24 The Maracanã Stadium

A	... is an architectural masterpiece.	
B	... was built right after the 1950 World Cup.	
C	... can accommodate up to 96 000 people.	
D	... became famous after Pelé's first goal.	

Q25 On sunny afternoons

A	... there are many BBQs on the beach.	
B	... Copacabana beach is jam-packed with Brazilian sporting stars.	
C	... Copacabana beach is used by people from different social backgrounds.	
D	... all of Rio is out in the sun, buying bikinis and shorts.	

[1] dampened: gedämpft

Q26 Many Brazilians

A	… practice nearly all year for their month-long Carnival street party.	
B	… are famous for their Swing and Jazz skills.	
C	… are admired by people all over the world for their ability to cope with the heat.	
D	… spend 11 month a year partying.	

Q27 The Sugarloaf

A	… should be visited in the evening.	
B	… should be visited in the morning.	
C	… is visited by huge crowds of people every evening.	
D	… can be crested with the help of an elevator.	

Q28 The writer of the article

A	… has a girlfriend called Susan.	
B	… married his girlfriend Jo in Brazil.	
C	… proposed to his girlfriend Jo.	
D	… split up with his girlfriend.	

6 points
(1 point each)

TIME FRAME
40 min

LISTENING TEST

Instructions:

1. This test contains 4 tasks and 34 questions.
2. Write all your answers in this test book.

Task 1

CD-TRACK 11

You are going to hear a report on technology. Listen carefully and then answer the questions (Q1–Q7) below by using a maximum of four words. Write your answers in the spaces provided. We have done the first example (0) for you.

0	What is the name of the daily radio feature presented by Lisa Williams?	**Five minutes a day**
Q1	What title did Sir Francis Bacon choose for his utopian novel that was published in 1624?	
Q2	What happened in 1818?	
Q3	What did the crew of Apollo 13 need creative solutions for?	
Q4	What was partly to blame for the oil catastrophe in the Gulf of Mexico?	
Q5	Which negative aspects of human life will people, according to Mr. Vance, not have to worry about any longer once they have merged with machines?	
Q6	Which species will humans get divided into once we have reached the era of The Singularity?	
Q7	What is the name of Lisa's male co-presenter?	

7 points
(1 point each)

Task 2

CD-TRACK 12

You are going to hear parts of a report called "In E-Books, Publishers Have Rivals: News Sites". You have 45 seconds to read the sentences below before the text will be played to you twice. While listening, choose the correct answer (A, B, C or D) for each question (Q8–Q12). Put an ✗ in the correct box. We have done the first example (0) for you. After you have listened to the text twice, you will have another 45 seconds to go through your answers again.

0 Amazon is

A	... a big publishing company.	
B	... getting less and less attractive.	
C	... one of the competitors of book publishers.	✗
D	... the only real competitor of book publishers.	

Q8 Nowadays, newspapers and magazines

A	... re-write existing e-books to create new versions of them.	
B	... publish e-books as well.	
C	... are threatened by the e-book market.	
D	... publish books, too.	

Q9 "Open Secret"

A	... is a non-fictional e-book that was published by the New York Times.	
B	... is a fictional e-book that was published by the New York Times.	
C	... is a highly unsuccessful non-fictional e-book.	
D	... is a successful fictional e-book.	

Q10 Stephan Rubin

A	... is the presenter and publisher of Holt & Company.	
B	... is an author whose books are published at Macmillan.	
C	... is good friends with the internationally renowned publisher Mr. Holt.	
D	... wrote a series of e-books on Rupert Murdoch.	

Q11 Random House is the name

A	... of the world's most famous publishing company.	
B	... of the first e-book ever.	
C	... was bought by Politico, a competing company.	
D	... of the world's biggest publisher.	

Q12 For the presidential race 2012

A	... four books will be published, each comprising 20,000 to 30,000 words.	
B	... four e-books are produced, each comprising 20,000 to 30,000 words.	
C	... four e-books will be written by Jon Meacham, an executive editor at Random House.	
D	... four books will be written by Jon Meacham, an executive editor at Random House.	

5 points
(1 point each)

Task 3

CD-TRACK 13

**You are going to hear parts of an interview about the new design of schools.
You have 45 seconds to read the sentences below before the text will be played to you twice. While listening, match the beginnings of the sentences (Q13–Q23) with the sentence endings (A–N). Write your answers in the table provided. There are two extra sentence endings that do not belong to the text at all. We have done the first example (0) for you.
After you have listened to the text twice, you will have another 45 seconds to go through your answers again.**

0	With regard to the design of new school buildings …
Q13	At the time of the radio interview …
Q14	Mr. Weyer's new design of school buildings is …
Q15	Traditional school buildings …
Q16	One of the new features is …
Q17	The development can be compared to …
Q18	The new school buildings are designed …
Q19	The radical idea of moving out of enclosed classrooms …
Q20	The teaching environment has an influence on …
Q21	Nowadays, a lot of teaching …
Q22	Students can bring their own laptops to these new schools …
Q23	As many simultaneous activities can take place in these new buildings, …

A	… Mr. Weyer was in Copenhagen.
B	… is group-based and interactive.
C	… a general trend towards larger and more flexible spaces can be observed.
D	… to meet the students' needs and help them find their individual ways of learning.
E	… how students learn.
F	… and can go online anywhere in the building.
G	… were structured around corridors that connected enclosed classrooms.
H	… was appreciated by teachers.
I	… the openness of the space.
J	… is based on new concepts in pedagogy.
K	… to a great extent based on the changes in teaching.
L	… what has happened to offices and office spaces.
M	… is based on the use of the black board.
N	… acoustics is one of the biggest challenges.

11 points
(1 point each)

0	Q13	Q14	Q15	Q16	Q17	Q18	Q19	Q20	Q21	Q22	Q23
C											

Task 4

CD-TRACK 14

You are going to hear parts of an audio guide through Central Park, New York City.
You have 45 seconds to read the sentences below before the text will be played to you twice. While listening, choose the correct answer (A, B, C or D) for each question (Q24–Q34). Put an ✗ in the correct box. We have done the first example (0) for you. After you have listened to the text twice, you will have another 45 seconds to go through your answers again.

0 Central Park

A	... is at the very heart of New York City.	✗
B	... is at the very heart of Paris.	
C	... is very hard to reach by New York Public Transport.	
D	... is situated in London's city centre.	

Q24 Central Park represents the perfect combination of

A	... green space and concrete space.	
B	... city design and rural planning and architecture.	
C	... landscape design, urban planning and architecture.	
D	... architectural ideas and countryside design.	

Q25 Central Park is

A	... dynamic like the other two big symbols of the city.	
B	... dynamic and therefore a different kind of symbol than the Statue of Liberty.	
C	... static like the Empire State Building.	
D	... one of the symbols of NYC, together with Times Square and the Statue of Liberty.	

Q26 Many New Yorkers feel the need

A	... to run away.	
B	... to be near something green and living.	
C	... to protect their park.	
D	... to water plants at Central Park.	

Q27 In order to enter Central Park

A	... you have to pay only a little fee.	
B	... you have to buy an expensive ticket.	
C	... you should get a ticket at one of the 20 gates.	
D	... you don't have to pay anything.	

Q28 In front of the Artist's Gate

A	... there are two statutes.	
B	... there are three statues.	
C	... there are four statues.	
D	... there is one statue.	

Q29 The Nature Sanctuary

A	... was restored in the 1980s.	
B	... was installed in the 1980s.	
C	... was closed down in 1934.	
D	... was closed down in 1980.	

Q30 Besides birds,

A	... mice and rats can be found in the Sanctuary.	
B	... woodpeckers and squirrels live in the Sancturay.	
C	... rabbits and woodchucks can be found in the Sanctuary.	
D	... the sanctuary also gives home to alley cats.	

Q31 The great models for Central Park

A	... were the public grounds in London and Paris.	
B	... were the private gardens in London and Paris.	
C	... was St. James Park in London.	
D	... was a private park in Paris.	

Q32 In former times,

A	... European pig farmers and gardeners used to live between 5th and 18th Avenue and 59th and 107th Street.	
B	... European pig farmers and gardeners used to live between 6th and 8th Avenue and 58th and 116th Street.	
C	... European pig farmers and gardeners used to live between 5th and 8th Avenue and 59th and 106th Street.	
D	... European pig farmers and gardeners used to live between 5th and 8th Avenue and 57th and 106th Street.	

Q33 At 8th Avenue and 82nd Street, there used to be

A	... a tiny African settlement without a church or a school.	
B	... a European settlement with three churches and a school.	
C	... an African-American settlement with two churches.	
D	... a big African-American settlement with three churches and even a school.	

Q34 Today Central Park is loved and especially used by

A	... joggers, inline roller skaters, nature lovers and bird watchers.	
B	... children.	
C	... adults of every social background.	
D	... New York City's high society.	

11 points
(1 point each)

TOTAL POINTS

Textnachweis

8–9: Peter Allen/Justin Davenport: £430 million art stolen in "heist of the century". In: London Evening Standard, 20th of May 2010, p. 1

10–11: Kevin Bradford: Sky's the limit – £85m Battle of Britain monument revealed. In: Hendon & Finchley Times, 20th of May 2010, p. 1

17: Christopher Dobbing: Our man in Iran. In: The Guardian, 16th of August 2008, Gap Year section, p. 5

19–20: Justine Southwick: Vietnam: Along the Mekong – A river runs through it. In: Venture, Issue 7, London, August 2010, p. 24

23: Information about Valencia from: http://www.enforex.com

24: Bishnu Sharma/Pam Dyer: Residents' involvement in tourism and their perceptions of tourism impacts. In: http://www.emeraldinsight.com

27–28: Christof Koch: When does consciousness arise? In the womb, at birth or during early childhood? In: Scientific American Mind, September/October 2009, p. 20

29–30: Graeme Paton: Schools forced to "mop up social problems". In: The Telegraph, 26th of July 2011

35–36: John Shepard-Barron: Entrepreneur who invented the automatic cash machine and spared the world six-figure PINs. In: The Daily Telegraph, 21st of May 2010, p. 35

38: Heide B. Malhotra: Keeping it in the family. In: The Epoch Times, 19th of May 2010, Business Section, p. 6

42/1: Data from: Eurostat

42/2: Ingrid Melander/Nicholas Vinocur: Germany warns of 'revolution' as youth unemployment threatens to tear Europe apart. In: http://financialpostbusiness.files.wordpress.com, 31st of May 2013

45–46: Haig Simonian: Charm, charisma and a sense of humour. In: The Financial Times, 11th of September 2011, Watches and Jewellery Section, p. 2

48–49: Katrin Bennhold: Women in Science See Risk and Reward. In: Standard, New York Times Section, 12th of July 2010, p. 3

52: Data from: Pew Internet Research (für alle Diagramme)

54–55: Andrew Pollack: Genetically Modified Fish Getting Closer to Tables. In: The New York Times, 26th of June 2010, p. A1

56–57: Hannah Wallace: In High Schools, a Critical Lens on Food. In: The New York Times, 27th of October 2011, p. A26

63: Data from: http://obesity-statistics.com

66–67: Jennifer Davies: Northern Exposure. In: The Guardian Gap Year Section, 16th of August 2008, p. 5

68–69: Hugh Pearman: Oxbridge, red-brick, plate-glass or new-wave universities – why your college is not simply a set of buildings. In: The Times, 20th of May 2010, p. 6

70–71: David Pogue: Tiny Screens Bearing Tiny Delights. In: The New York Times, 11th of August 2011, p. B1

72–73: Benoit Denizet-Lewis: It's Not U. It's Me. In: The New York Times Sunday Magazine, 7th of August 2011, p. MM14

80–81: Gia Kourlas: Hip-Hop, Folk and Karate Through a Strainer on a Hot Afternoon. In: The New York Times, 15th of August 2011, p. C4

82–83: Jenna Wortham: As Networks Speed Up, Data Hits a Wall. In: The New York Times, 15th of August 2011, p. B1

84–85: Jenny Anderson: For a Standout College Essay, Applicants Fill Their Summers. In: The New York Times, 6th of August 2011, p. A1

86–87: Rob Smith: Nuts about Brazil. In: Venture, Explore your world, Issue 7, p. 22

Textnachweis und Titelverzeichnis Audio-CD

Track-Nr.	Zeit	Titel/Musikstück	Urheber	Quelle
1	04:04	Imagine Art After		http://www.guardian.co.uk © Guardian News & Media Ltd 2011
2 – 1	01:15	New York State of Mind	T. u. M.: Billy Joel	Billy Joel: Turnstiles © 1976 Sony Music Entertainment Inc.
2 – 2	01:17	Leaving on a jet plane	T. u. M.: John Denver	John Denver: John Denver's Greatest Hits. (P) 2005 SONY BMG MUSIC ENTERTAINMENT
2 – 3	00:45	Molly Malone	T.: James Yorkston	The Dubliners: alive – alive – o © 2008 IML Irish Music Licensing Ltd.
3	05:12	Radio show on the importance of play for children		http://sic.conversationsnetwork.org
4	05:58	Radio show on Curricula Vitae	Niki Chestworth	Get your CV noticed. In: The London Evening Standard, 20th of May 2010, p. 50
5	03:49	Radio show on artificial life	Fred Attewill	Dr. God creates artificial life in lab. In: Metro, 21st of Mai 2010, p. 1
6	05:05	Radio show „Please Explain"		http://www.wnyc.org; Stand 16.1.2009
7	02:17	Report on a football academy	Ales Hayes	Football academy kicks off. In: Hendon & Finchley Times, 20th of May 2010, p. 11
8	05:07	Interview with country singer Mr. Chesney	David Pogue	Country Singer, Songwriter and C.E.O. In: The New York Times, 13th of August 2011, p. BBU2
9	03:58	Interview about African Art		http://www.metmuseum.org
10	03:40	Audio guide through one of London's districts		Excerpted from Rick Steves' London guidebook and audio tours app, with permission from the author. Learn more at www.ricksteves.com
11	04:08	Report on technology	Kevin Delaney	Technology, leaving humanity behind. In: The New York Times (articles selected for Der Standard), 15th of July 2010, p. 1
12	03:54	Report called „In E-Books, Publishers Have Rivals: News Sites"	Julie Bosman/ Jeremy W. Peters	In E-Books, Publishers Have Rivals: News Sites. In: The New York Times, 19th of September 2011, p. B1
13	04:53	Interview about the new design of schools		World Architecture News; http://www.worldarchitecturenews.com
14	05:47	Audio guide through Central Park		http://www.centralpark.com

Summe Zeit: 01:01:09